To Tommy

HAPPY 12th BIRTHDAY

FROM YOUR GRANDFATHER

Norb

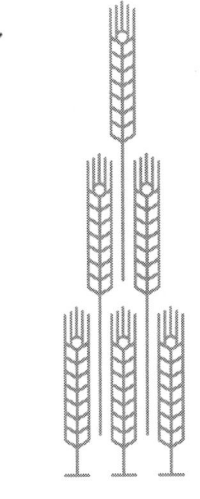

Life's Harvest

Norb Svanascini

DEDICATION

I dedicate this book to my Wife,

who has been my loyal friend since we were 11 years old.

To my Children:

Elizabeth, Michael, and Anthony.

And my Grandchildren:

Joe, Andrew, Steve, Nick, Alex, Frank, Paul, Tommy, and Billy.

The Library of Congress Cataloging-in-Publication Data is available upon request.

ISBN 978-0-9994083-0-8

First Edition: September 2017

THANKS

I have many people to thank in the writing of this book, but special thanks goes to my grandchildren Alex and Frank Svanascini, Dragan Mitrovic, the graphic artist that put his heart in designing the cover, and last but not least to Nadine Rayahin, who had the patience to work with my disorganized manner, and amazingly, organized it.

TABLE OF CONTENTS

If you get anything else from this book, this poem by Kipling to his son on his 16th birthday is the one thing you should cherish; in my mind, the greatest thing ever written for any young person, and something that should be required to be recited at every graduation.

Norb Svanascini

If

By Rudyard Kipling

If you ca keep your head when all about you
Are losing theirs and blaming it on you;
If you can trust yourself when all men doubt you,
But make allowance for their doubting too:
If you can wait and not be tired by waiting,
Or, being lied about, don't deal in lies,
Or being hated don't give way to hating,
And yet don't look too good, nor talk too wise;

If you can dream - and not make dreams your master;
If you can think - and not make thoughts your aim,
If you can meet with Triumph and Disaster
And treat those two impostors just the same.
If you can bear to hear the truth you've spoken
Twisted by knaves to make a trap for fools,
Or watch the things you gave your life to, broken,

And stoop and build'em up with worn-out tools;
If you can make one heap of all your winnings
And risk it on one turn of pitch-and-toss,
And lose, and start again at your beginnings,
And never breathe a word about your loss:
If you can force your heart and nerve and sinew
To serve your turn long after they are gone,
And so hold on when there is nothing in you
Except the Will which says to them: "Hold on!"

If you can talk with crowds and keep your virtue,
Or walk with Kings - nor lose the common touch,
If neither foes nor loving friends can hurt you,
If all men count with you, but none too much:
If you can fill the unforgiving minute
With sixty seconds' worth of distance run,
Yours is the Earth and everything that's in it,
And - which is more - you'll be a Man, my son!

WHY THIS BOOK?

I want to leave something of value to my family, especially my grandchildren, and hoping that others might get some value from the collection of stories, and quotes that I have accumulated throughout my lifetime.

I hope these stories and quotes make you THINK, especially in today's world where independent thinking is not in vogue.

We must all remember Socrates when he told us to believe in nothing until we have examined all possibilities, discard the senseless ones, and keep the logical ones.

Remember: You were given a mind to THINK, not to believe something just because someone told you so. This is what separates humans from all other species.

One of the first deep thoughts I had was when my father was employed by the wealthiest man in the town I grew up in. The same town also had a major University.

My father was invited to join his employer as well as the President of the University in the town's country club.

My father invited me to go with him. Being a teenager at that time,

I remember the University President, an extremely educated man, who was even an advisor to Presidents, asking me what I was interested in. When you are 15 or 16 there are a few things that boys are really passionate about but a common one is cars.

When I mentioned my love of cars and how much I loved working with them, he made a comment that I reflect to this day: "I know nothing about cars; in fact, I am useless when it comes to anything mechanical."

It dawned on me, and seemed strange why society gives more credence and respect to a person who knows more details of Charlemagne's history than a mechanic or a plumber.

Looking at this man, and also knowing a lot of so-called "mechanical inclined people," I had no problem deciding who I would prefer to be with on a deserted island.

I've also given a lot of thoughts about my wife and our children's mother, Charlene. She, like a lot of wives, has given so much to create and support families, that society takes them for granted.

Just to give you an idea of what my wife (and many others, of course) has done while raising 3 children, I'll give you some examples:

In the three years of diaper changing: over 3,000 diaper changes.

In the 20 years of children living at home: around 22,000 meals.

Wash loads: around 18,000.

Plus cleaning house, taking children to school, etc., etc.
There is no woman that will love you like your mother.

Thank her.

I have always been influenced by movies; as a child growing up in a country that had no television I was influenced and formed by going to the movie theater and seeing three movies at a time, shorts and also cartoons.

I sincerely believe that the movie industry created the greatest art form ever devised by man. I'm sure many people are awed by looking at the Mona Lisa, but compared to the amount of people that have been moved by watching Bambi or Casablanca or it's a Wonderful Life, it doesn't even compare.

For a long time when America was really the moral beacon of the world, and it showed that the righteous person always came through was the winner, no matter whether it was John Wayne, Alan Ladd, or Gary Cooper. The person watching the movie at least had a moral compass that they could follow.

After every chapter in this book I want to include recommendations of movies about the subject.

I hope that these will aid you about what to do, and also give you some kind of a guide that will remain with you all your life.

FOREWORD

It was in June of 1953 that I arrived to this country from Argentina. My father was a radio/TV engineer and was brought here by a gentleman who had a TV tuner factory. Upon arrival in Miami, where we had to bring chest x-rays to show we were healthy, we were questioned. Not only were we questioned about his job but also on the subject of our understanding about what this country stood for and explaining that we could become citizens after 5 years if we were good and law abiding.

My father had to sign a promise to the US Government that he would never be a burden to the United States and his employer had to guarantee my father's promise.

We moved to Bloomington, Indiana and lived there for 10 years.

The U.S. at that time was a really incredible place and something you couldn't understand if you didn't experience it. To remind you of some things, I'll quickly tell you.

You didn't lock the doors of your home.

I never heard anyone talk bad about a black person. In fact, if they were hard working, there was an aura of protection and respect towards that family that was promoted by everyone.

I went to a regular high school that taught a semester of woodworking, auto shop, mechanical drawing, printing, and even agriculture. Teachers were respected, we had a dress code, every kid worked, and every kid bought their own car. Television had Jackie Gleason, Sid Caesar, Father Knows Best, and Andy Griffith.

There really were no drugs and there was an unwritten feeling that this really was the way to live.

The cars were Buicks, Fords, Chevrolets, Chryslers, and Nashs. No foreign names. The Radios and TVs were Zenith, Admiral, Sylvania, and Philco. Again, no foreign names as everything was made in America.

People trusted each other, people were proud to be Americans, and people KNEW what the right thing to do was even if they didn't do it.

I have lived in this country since then and, thanks to my Father's love for this country, I also continue the family tradition of not being able to hold back the tears whenever I visit the Jefferson Memorial or Mount Vernon. I read the words that those magnificent men wrote and, most importantly, practiced.

Not many Nations last long if the foundation that they were created upon is eroded. Little by little, but for sure, it will collapse.

In the last 60+ years we have eroded this Republic to the point that no child is taught American history. Just think, our own children are not taught about the greatest social system ever put on this earth and it belongs to them, just like their parents belong to them.

I cannot understand why we don't protect these ideals like rabid dogs. In fact, in these last few years, it's almost a sin to defend the constitution or not to abide by the "politically correct" stance that happens to be in style at that moment.

Just look around you, you are surrounded by armies of takers and whiners that live for the moment without any regard to the ideals of America. Our politicians are nothing more than wind socks to determine what is in style today so they can be re-elected. Our schools are a joke. Even in these "institutes of learning", PC is the most important subject. Who decides what is politically correct, anyway?

Can you believe that in these years if someone crosses the border into this country illegally and they have "rights" that you, the real citizen, have to pay for them? Who decided that?

I love the ideals of the founding fathers of this country and I want them back. I do not want politically correct jibber jabber that some idealistic idiot thought of.

You should be mad as hell, your grandchildren will ask, "How did my grandparents let this happen?"

I'm ending this by enclosing a tribute to people that understood the principles that were the foundation of America.

I envy them.

Our Heritage and Legacy
The Cost of Freedom

Only two people signed the Declaration of Independence on July 4th: John Hancock and Charles Thomson. Most of the rest signed on August 2nd, but the last signature wasn't added until 5 years later.

Have you ever wondered what happened to the 56 men who signed the Declaration of Independence?

Five signers were captured by the British as traitors and tortured before they died.

Twelve had their homes ransacked and burned.

Two lost their sons serving in the Revolutionary Army; another had two sons captured.

Nine of the 56 fought and died from wounds or hardships of the Revolutionary War.

What kind of men were they?

Twenty-four were lawyers and jurists. Eleven were merchants, nine were farmers and large plantation owners; men of means, well educated.

But they signed the Declaration of Independence knowing full well that the penalty would be death if they were captured.

Carter Braxton of Virginia, a wealthy planter and trader, saw his ships swept from the seas by the British Navy. He sold his home and properties to pay his debts and died in rags.

Thomas McKeam was so hounded by the British that he was forced to move his family almost constantly. He served in the Congress without pay and his family was kept in hiding. His possessions were taken from him and poverty was his reward.

Vandals or soldiers looted the properties of Dillery, Hall, Clymer, Walton, Gwinnett, Heyward, Ruttledge, and Middleton. At the battle of Yorktown, Thomas Nelson Jr. noted that British General Cornwallis had taken over the Nelson home for his headquarters. He quietly urged General George Washington to open fire. The home was destroyed and Nelson died bankrupt.

Francis Lewis had his home and properties destroyed. The enemy jailed his wife and she died within a few months.

John Hart was driven from his wife's bedside as she was dying. Their 13 children fled for their lives. His fields and his gristmill were laid to waste. For more than a year, he lived in forests and caves and returned home to find his wife dead and his children vanished. A few weeks later, he died from exhaustion and a broken heart. Norris and Livingston suffered similar fates. Such were the stories and sacrifices of the American Revolution.

These were not wild-eyed, rabble-rousing ruffians. They were soft-spoken men of means and education. They had security, but they valued liberty more. Standing tall, straight, and unwavering, they pledged: "For the support of this Declaration, with firm reliance on the protection of the Divine Providence, we mutually pledge to each other, our Lives, our Fortunes, and our sacred Honor."

The history books never tell a lot about what happened in the Revolutionary War. We didn't fight only the British. We were British subjects at that time and we fought our own government! Some of us take these liberties so much for granted, but we shouldn't. So, take a few minutes while enjoying your 4th of July holiday and silently thank these patriots. It's not much to ask for the price they paid.

"The Americans combine the notions of Christianity and of liberty so intimately in their minds, that it is impossible to make them conceive the one without the other."

"In France I had almost always seen the spirit of religion and the spirit of freedom marching in opposite directions. But in America I found they were intimately united and that they reigned in common over the same country."

"I sought for the key to the greatness and genius of America in her harbors…; in her fertile fields and boundless forests; in her rich mines and vast world commerce; in her public school system and institutions of learning. I sought for it in her democratic Congress and in her matchless Constitution. Not until I went into the churches of America and heard her pulpits flame with righteousness did I understand the secret of her genius and power."

"America is great because America is good, and if America ever ceases to be good, America will cease to be great."

Alex de Tocqueville on America

THOUGHTS

Walt Disney's
Think, Believe, Dream, and Dare

This is a story about a man who has had an impact on the lives of millions of people all over the world.
Mr. Walt Disney

One day a group of third and fourth graders took a field trip to Walt Disney World in Orlando, Florida. They spent most of the morning walking around, seeing the sights, going on rides, etc. They were getting ready to go, when Walt Disney met them at Snow White's Wishing Well and asked the children if they had any questions for him. The students replied:

"Mr. Disney! Mr. Disney! How did you ever think of Mickey Mouse?"
"Mr. Disney! How do you that voice for Donald Duck?"
"Mr. Disney! Why are there seven dwarfs instead of ten?" (Etc...)

Finally, after a number of curious questions, Mr. Disney said, "All right children, we have time for one final question before you leave." With that he notice a little third grade girl tugging gently at his pant leg. She asked:

"Mr. Disney, if you had the opportunity to tell every child/person in the entire world one thing, what would it be?"

Mr. Disney thought for a moment and looked down at the small child and said,

"If I had the opportunity I would tell every child/person in the world just four words. These words are posted right beside my bed. I read them every morning when I wake up. I read them every night before I go to bed. These words are: think, believe, dream, and dare."

THINK: The first word is Think. You need to think about the morals and values that you want to live your life by. Your parents have done an excellent job in guiding you and developing your morals and values. You need to take what you have learned and decide for yourselves what the type of person you want to be, Now who out here heard of the story, "The Little Engine that Could?" That story has an important meaning. That little engine was going up that huge hill saying, "I think I can, I think I can, I think I can." And that positive attitude enabled him to get over the hill and deliver all of the presents to the boys and girls in the valley below. So not only do you need to think about what kind of person you want to be, you need to also think positively about that person.

BELIEVE: The second word is Believe. All of us out here need to believe in many things. You need to believe in your friends, your family, your faith, etc... But the most important person that you need to believe in is yourself. You need to believe in what you set out to do in your life. Incorporate whatever beliefs pertain to your situation.

DREAM: The third word that Mr. Disney said was Dream. Dreaming is the creative word, you can dream to be anything you want to be in life. You can dream to be doctor, lawyer, (etc.). But the most important thing to remember - the bigger you dream, the further you go,

DARE: The fourth and final word that Mr. Disney said was Dare. Dare is the action word. It is important to think, believe and dream, but daring is where you go out and get things done. As we all know there are good dares and bad dares. You will have to make decisions throughout your life based on dares. But, if you believe in what you think and dream to be, daring yourself to do the right thing will come naturally.

So remember Walt Disney and his four words – think, believe, dream, and dare – as you continue along your journey called life.

"The darkest hour in any man's life is when he sits down to plan how to get money without earning it."

Horace Greeley

"Some of us will do our jobs well and some will not, but we will all be judged by only one thing – the results."

Vincent Lombardi

The most important of all our perceptions is the way we perceive ourselves. There is a story in American Indian folklore that illustrates this truth very clearly. According to the legend, an Indian brave came upon an eagle's egg which had somehow fallen unbroken from an eagle's nest. Unable to find the nest, the brave put the egg in the nest of a prairie chicken, where it is proverbial strong eyes, saw the world for the first time. Looking at the other prairie chickens, he did what they did. He crawled and scratched at the earth, pecked here and there for stray grains and husks, now and then rising in a flutter a few feet above the earth and then descending again. He accepted and imitated the daily routine of the earthbound prairie chickens. And he spent most of his life this way.

Then, as the story continues, one day an eagle flew over the brood of prairie chickens. The now aging eagle, who still thought he was a prairie chicken, looked up in awed admiration as the great bird soared through the skies. "What is that?" he gasped in astonishment. One of the old prairie chickens replied, "I have seen one before. That is the eagle, the proudest, strongest, and most magnificent of all the bird. But don't you ever dream that you could be like that. You are like the rest of us and we are prairie chickens." And so, shackled by this belief, the eagle lived and died thinking he was a prairie chicken.

Our lives are shaped by the way we perceive ourselves. The all-important attitudes by which we perceive and evaluate ourselves tell us who we are and describe the appropriate behavior for such a person. We live and die according to our self-perception.

The Christian Vision

"If we could see the miracle of a single flower clearly, our whole life would change"

Buddha

"The only thing worse than being blind is having sight but no vision."

Helen Keller

"Men never do evil so completely and cheerfully as when they do it from religious conviction."

Blaise Pascal

"In individuals, insanity is rare; but in groups, parties, nations, and epochs it is the rule."

Fredrich Nietzsche

The object of living is work, experience, happiness. There is joy in work. All that money can do is buy us someone else's work in exchange for our own. There is no happiness except in the realization that we have accomplished something.

Henry Ford

"But if any provide not for his own, and specially for those of his own house, he hath denied the faith, and is worse than an infidel."

1 Timothy 5:8

"Everything is easy once someone shows you how."

Christopher Columbus

When I was a boy of fourteen, my father was so ignorant I could hardly stand to have the old man around. But when I got to twenty-one, I was astonished at how much he had learned in seven years.

Mark Twain

"Winning is a habit. Unfortunately, so is losing."

Vince Lombardi

"If you pick up a starving dog and make him prosperous, he will not bite you. This is the principal difference between a dog and a man."

Mark Twain

"A witty saying proves nothing."

Voltaire

"It's a greater sin to kill someone's mind, than to kill the person itself."
Norb Svanascini

"I would rather be a person in jail with a free mind, than out of jail, with a mind in prison."

Norb Svanascini

"Ninety percent of the friction of life is caused by the tone of voice."
Arnold Bennet

Him that I love, I wish to be free -- even from me.
Anne Morrow Lindbergh

Though I do not believe that a plant will spring up where no seed has been, I have great faith in a seed. Convince me that you have a seed there, and I am prepared to expect wonders.

Henry David Thoreau

"Don't judge each day by the harvest you reap, but by the seeds that you plant."

Robert Louis Stevenson

"When I do good I feel good, when I do bad I feel bad, and that's my religion."

Abe Lincoln

"Never spend your money before you have it."

Thomas Jefferson

"When you're good at what you do, corruption is unnecessary."

Anthony Svanascini

"He who is his own friend, is a friend to all men."

Seneca

SNOW

I pity the person who has never seen snow;
I pity more the person who has seen it and does not appreciate it.
Snow is God's way to paint his creation.
Snow is fair, it's clean, pure, and most of all, it's peaceful.
Snow is for the poor and for the rich, for child and adult.
But most of all, it's really, really white.

Norb Svanascini

"It is the soul and not the strong-box which should be filled."

Seneca

There once was a little boy who was born blind. His mother never really recovered from the shock of realizing her son would never see.

When the boy was ten, he was walking with his mother when he suddenly exclaimed: What a beautiful day! What fresh air, can you smell the flowers? Can you hear the birds singing?

His mother, with tears in her eyes said to him: I'm so sorry you cannot see these things as they are so beautiful.

And the son replied: Mother, I do not need to see to appreciate the beauty of the world you see. I believe in all those beautiful things because I feel them just as I feel the greater force that created all these things and no one has seen it either.

Norb Svanascini

PAULINA'S KITCHEN

Many years ago, as a young child in another country, I grew up in a very close family atmosphere. My fondest memories were of my grandmother's kitchen. It was a very large kitchen, with a large stove, a huge table and a huge working area where my four cousins and I would spend almost every Sunday while my grandmother made from scratch those wonderful dinners where all her four children, their husbands and wives, and their children would come to eat.

My grandmother was a very short woman, whose girth almost matched her stature. She was an old fashioned grandmother, which meant that if you misbehaved, she would not hesitate to spank you, but in ten minutes she would hug and kiss you in such a way, that you knew, that she really loved and cared for you so much, that the spankings weren't a punishment as much as to teach you right from wrong.

The kitchen walls were covered with tile, and she would allow us to cut up comic books, wet the pictures, and stick them to the tiles all over, so when they dried, there would be these pictures all over the kitchen; in between she would be making the flat pasta for the lower part of the ravioli, then she would prepare the intricate meat filling which was passed from mother to daughter for generations. The top layer of pasta came last, and this was the moment the grandkids looked forward to.

She would take the ravioli wheel, and take each granchild's hand inside hers and guided it so the lines required to achieve that perfect square, would not veer from its course; after making sure that we all had an equal amount of time doing this, she would kiss us all with that face covered and smelling like flour.

The best compliment the family could give her while eating was to be silent and say nothing as we were enjoying this feast, as her biggest pleasure was to say to everybody : "No one is talking, the food must be good".

We left the country of my birth and moved to the United States when I was 11 years old. It's not easy for anybody to move to another country, another society, but it's not as hard for a young person.

I remembered everyone form my homeland once in a while, but the one person I remembered the most was my grandmother; I never knew, nor have I ever met such a wise person; this woman who only went to the second grade, knew more about life, had more common sense, than anyone I've ever met.

I've always wondered, in this age of the emancipated woman, trying to justify their life with a so called career, leaving their children at day care centers, if any one of them will ever achieve what my grandmother achieved, the remembrance of her with tears in our eyes, of her fairness of her love, of creating a memory to be respected until we pass on.

I saw her once more when she came to the U.S. to visit us, she stayed for one month, and after that I visited my homeland when I was nineteen, which is an age where you are not really in an appreciative mood.

I never saw her again, she died, like all people die, but the longer I live the more I think about her in that kitchen, probably the happiest spot I've ever been in.

After a 30 year absence, I went back to visit the country I was born in, and went to my grandmother's house which is now my aunt's where she lives with her two sons. I went into the kitchen; it measured 7x8 feet. I asked my aunt if it had been remodeled, or another room made larger so it took away from the size of the kitchen-she replied: "No, it's the same size----It always looked bigger when she was here didn't it?

Norb Svanascini

Why isn't there a Harvard or Princeton or Yale for sports where the graduates would automatically be the best athletes? Because there's no bullshit in sports. The results in that area are provable by performance not by how much your daddy made, or how important your family is, or how much money you donate.

Norb Svanascini

"Talk is cheap and it works in politics. In the real world, the idea must actually work."

Norb Svanascini

MY LIFE CLOSED TWICE BEFORE ITS CLOSE

My life closed twice before its close—
It yet remains to see
If Immortality unveil
A third event to me

So huge, so hopeless to conceive
As these that twice befell.
Parting is all we know of heaven,
And all we need of hell.

Emily Dickinson

It Couldn't Be Done

Somebody said that it couldn't be done,
But he with a chuckle replied
That "maybe it couldn't," but he would be one
Who wouldn't say so till he'd tried.
So he buckled right in with the trace of a grin
On his face. If he worried he hid it.
He started to sing as he tackled the thing
That couldn't be done, and he did it.

Somebody scoffed: "Oh, you'll never do that;
At least no one ever has done it";
But he took off his coat and he took off his hat,
And the first thing we knew he'd begun it.
With a lift of his chin and a bit of a grin,
Without any doubting or quiddit,
He started to sing as he tackled the thing
That couldn't be done, and he did it.

There are thousands to tell you it cannot be done,
There are thousands to prophesy failure;
There are thousands to point out to you, one by one,
The dangers that wait to assail you.
But just buckle in with a bit of a grin,
Just take off your coat and go to it;
Just start to sing as you tackle the thing
That "cannot be done," and you'll do it.

Edgar Guest

"My best friend is the one who brings out the best in me."

Henry Ford

"If you speak when angry, you'll make the best speech you'll ever regret."

Groucho Marx

The truth of the matter is that there are only two kinds of people in the world: the ones who actually produce something and the ones who live off the producers. For some unknown reason (except for the obvious one of just plain hatred towards people who get rich by actually making something), people pay a lot of money and respect for unproven theories held mostly by charlatans that are self-promoting in these unprovable fields all the way from the learning centers to government. As an example, you couldn't live without farmers or plumbers but you wouldn't miss in a lifetime an economist or psychiatrist. Inversely, farmers and plumbers are paid little and respected less than economists or psychiatrists.

Politics is at the top of this heap. Almost all societies collapse from the encroachment and avarice of politicians; from European royalty which serves the same purpose as a soap opera, to our esteemed current politicians and their want for more and more of non-producing waste whether from studying growth of algae in the archipelago of Chile, to redistributing monies from producer to non-producer, guarantees the ultimate destruction of societies. There seems to be a correlation between the gift of gab and admiration by the populace.

I had the pleasure of listening to a very famous singer, and the double pleasure of having dinner with him, and it occurred to me; why is it that a person that has the gift of gab is automatically thought of by the people, that this person would make a good politician? Doesn't it make as much sense as a good singer would make a good politician or president? President Elvis Presley, President Michael Jackson, has a nice ring, doesn't it? Isn't it just as ridiculous to think that because somebody can read a written speech, qualifies this person to lead the public? Just think, throughout history, people are chosen for being good charlatans and, for this, they are giving access to unimaginable sums of monies so they can disperse it to the other charlatans. Like a friend of mine always says: The Axis that the world revolves around is made out of bullshit.

Norb Svanascini

The Modern 4 Horsemen of the Apocalypse

Politics - Religion - Media - Academia

These 4 horsemen are advancing through society in concentrated and united manner that destroys anything in its way, and if one of these 4 gets maimed or injured, the other three increase their efforts in such a way , that the total thrust of their crusade is not diminished.

Norb Svanascini

Youth is not a time of life. It is a state of mind. It is a test of the will, a quality of imagination, vigor of emotions, and a predominance of courage over timidity, of the appetite for adventure over love of ease. Nobody grows old by merely living a number of years. People grow old only by deserting their ideals. Years wrinkle the skin, but to give up enthusiasm wrinkles the soul. Worry, doubt, self-distrust, fear and despair ... these are the quick equivalents of the long, long years that bow the head and turn the growing spirit back to dust. Whether 70 or 16 there is, in every being' s heart, the love of wonder, the sweet amazement of the stars, and the star like things and thought, the undaunted challenge of events; the unfailing childlike appetite for 'what next?' You are as young as your faith, as old as your doubt, as young as your self-confidence, as old as your fear, as young as your hope, as old as your despair. So long as your heart receives messages of beauty, cheer, courage, grandeur and power from the earth, from man and from the Infinite, so long are you young. When all the wires are down, and all the central places of your heart are covered with the snows of pessimism and the ice of cynicism, then, and only then, are you grown old indeed, and may God have mercy on your soul.

General MacArthur

"You can put lipstick and earrings on a pig, and call her Peggy Sue, but it's still a pig."

Texas wisdom

Red Marbles

During the waning years of the depression in a small Idaho community, I used to stop by Mr. Miller's roadside stand for farm fresh produce as the season made it available. Food and money were still extremely scarce and bartering was used extensively.

One day Mr. Miller was bagging some early potatoes for me. I noticed a small boy, delicate of bone and feature, ragged but clean, hungrily appraising a basket of freshly picked green peas. I paid for my potatoes but was also drawn to the display of fresh green peas. I am a pushover for creamed peas and new potatoes. Pondering the peas, I couldn't help overhearing the conversation between Mr. Miller and the ragged boy next to me. "Hello Barry, how are you today?"

"H'lo, Mr. Miller. Fine, thank ya. Jus' admirin' them peas ... sure look good."
"They are good, Barry. How's your Ma?""Fine. Gittin' stronger alla' time."

"Good. Anything I can help you with?" "No, Sir. Jus' admirin' them peas."

"Would you like to take some home?" "No, Sir. Got nuthin' to pay for 'em with."

"Well, what have you to trade me for some of those peas?" "All I got's my prize marble here." "Is that right? Let me see it." "Here 'tis. She's a dandy."

"I can see that. Hmmmmm, only thing is this one is blue and I sort of go for red. Do you have a red one like this at home?" "Not zackley ... but almost."

"Tell you what. Take this sack of peas home with you and next trip this way let me look at that red marble." "Sure will. Thanks Mr. Miller."

Mrs. Miller, who had been standing nearby, came over to help me. With a smile she said, "There are two other boys like him in our community, all three are in very poor circum-stances. Jim just loves to bargain with them for peas, apples, tomatoes, or whatever. When they come back with their red marbles, and they always do, he decides he doesn't like red after all and he sends them home with a bag of produce for a green marble or an orange one, perhaps."

I left the stand smiling to myself, impressed with this man. A short time later I moved to Colorado but I never forgot the story of this man, the boys, and their bartering. Several years went by, each more rapid that the previous one.

Just recently I had occasion to visit some old friends in that Idaho community and while I was there learned that Mr. Miller had died. They were having his viewing that evening and knowing my friends wanted to go, I agreed to accompany them. Upon arrival at the mortuary we fell into line to meet the relatives of the deceased and to offer whatever words of comfort we could.

Ahead of us in line were three young men. One was in an army uniform and the other two wore nice haircuts, dark suits and white shirts ... all very professional looking. They approached Mrs. Miller, standing composed and smiling by her husband's casket. Each of the young men hugged her, kissed her on the cheek, spoke briefly with her and moved on to the casket. Her misty light blue eyes followed them as, one by one, each young man stopped briefly and placed his own warm hand over the cold pale hand in the casket.

Each left the mortuary awkwardly, wiping his eyes. Our turn came to meet Mrs. Miller. I told her who I was and mentioned the story she had told me about the marbles. With her eyes glistening, she took my hand and led me to the casket."Those three young men who just left were the boys I told you about. They just told me how they appreciated the things Jim "traded" them. Now, at last, when Jim could not change his mind about color or size ... they came to pay their debt."

"We've never had a great deal of the wealth of this world," she confided, "but right now, Jim would consider himself the richest man in Idaho."

With loving gentleness she lifted the lifeless fingers of her deceased husband. Resting underneath were three exquisitely shined red marbles.

Moral: We will not be remembered by our words, but by our kind deeds.

Life is not measured by the breaths we take, but by the moments that take our breath.

By W. E. Petersen

Today ...

I wish you a day of ordinary miracles ...
A fresh pot of coffee you didn't make yourself
An unexpected phone call from an old friend
Green stoplights on your way to work
The fastest line at the grocery store
A good sing-along song on the radio
Your keys right where you left them

Author Unknown

You become what you think about.

Earl Nightingale

Recommended Movies

Bambi
The Wizard of Oz
Pinocchio
Captain Courageous
Citizen Kane
Gone with the Wind

CHAPTER 2

GOVERNMENT

"In politics, an absurdity is not a handicap."

"If you wish to be a success in the world, promise everything, deliver nothing."

Napoleon Bonaparte

The fight for justice against corruption is never easy. It never has been and never will be. It exacts a toll on our self, our families, our friends, and especially our children. In the end, I believe, as in my case, the price we pay is well worth holding on to our dignity.

Frank Serpico

"Governments are the domain of the parasites of humanity."

Norb Svanascini

I don't want your help, unless you want to help me.
I don't want you to worry about my education.
I don't want you to worry about my health.
I'll take care of myself,
This is what I am,
This is what I want to be,
You see, I'm an American,
And my forefathers didn't come here for a handout.
They left their countries where governments
Made their decisions for them.
It's our duty to protect that heritage,
Those ideals of freedom,
Not a return to what they ran away from.

Norb Svanascini

Find out just what any people will quietly submit to and you have found out the exact measure of injustice and wrong which will be imposed upon them, and these will continue till they are resisted with either words or blows, or with both. The limits of tyrants are prescribed by the endurance of those whom they oppress.

Frederick Douglas

"Politicians are like diapers; they need to be changed often and for the same reason"

Mark Twain

"Remove justice, and what are kingdoms but gangs of criminals on a large scale? What are criminal gangs but petty kingdoms? A gang is a group of men under the command of a leader, bound by a compact of association, in which the plunder is divided according to an agreed convention.

If this villainy wins so many recruits from the ranks of the demoralized that it acquires territory, establishes a base, captures cities and subdues peoples, it then openly arrogates to itself the title of kingdom, which is conferred on it in the eyes of the world, not by the renouncing of aggression but by the attainment of impunity."

St. Augustine of Hippo

On September 19, 2008 the world entered a new era. Up to now monies were to be backed by something, this backing being gold, silver, or an asset that could be described, as a home, land, etc.

Today, however, we entered an era where the biggest asset creating instrument is a magic computer. Yes, a computer in which, by punching a new set of numbers, say a trillion, a new asset is created magically, where any entity which has made ridiculous investments can now dip into and instantly not made responsible for its irresponsibility.

What a difference this would have made for our forefathers. Instead of warning us about the irresponsibility of bankers and making sure that our money was backed by gold or silver as our Constitution demands, they could have put in use this magic computer as the bottomless pit of money creativity that would make every citizen of the United States not only very wealthy but also totally freed from any responsibility.

Norb Svanascini

Governments can only be controlled by the issuing of sound money. People, who produce nothing, must invent ways to get money with smoke and mirrors. This is what the Federal Reserve really is, 'Smoke and Mirrors'.

Societies that build their foundations on sand, have no other future than the collapse of what they've built.

Norb Svanascini

Gentlemen, I have had men watching you for a long time, and I am convinced that you have used the funds of the bank to speculate in the breadstuffs of the country. When you won, you divided the profits amongst you, and when you lost, you charged it to the bank. You tell me that if I take the deposits from the bank and annul its charter, I shall ruin ten thousand families. That may be true, gentlemen, but that is your sin! Should I let you go on, you will ruin fifty thousand families, and that would be my sin! You are a den of vipers and thieves. I intend to rout you out, and by the Eternal God, I will rout you out.

Andrew Jackson
to a delegation of bankers – 1834

"I've always believed that America's government was a unique political system one designed by geniuses so it could be run by idiots. I was wrong. No system can be smart enough to survive this level of incompetence and recklessness by the people charged to run it."

Thomas Friedman

I was talking to a friend of mine's little girl, and she said she wanted to be President someday. Both of her parents, confirmed liberals, were standing there, so I asked her, "If you were President what would be the first thing you would do?" She replied, "I'd give food and houses to all the homeless people."

"Wow - what a worthy goal." I told her, "You don't have to wait until you're President to do that. You can come over to my house and mow, pull weeds, and sweep my yard, and I'll pay you $50. Then I'll take you over to the grocery store where a homeless guy hangs out, and you can give him the $50 to use toward food or a new house." She thought that over for a few seconds 'cause she's only 6. And while her Mom glared at me, the little girl looked me straight in the eye and asked, "Why doesn't the homeless guy come over and do the work, and you can just pay him the $50?" And I said, "Welcome to Conservatism."
Her folks still aren't talking to me.

Unknown

A great civilization is not conquered from without until it has destroyed itself within. The essential causes of Rome's decline lay in her people, her morals, her class struggle, her falling trade, her bureaucratic despotism, her stifling taxes, her consuming wars. The political causes of decay were rooted in one fact - that increasing despotism destroyed the citizen's civic sense, and dried up statesmanship at its source.

Dr. Will Durant
The Story of Civilization, Vol.111

"In a Republic this rule ought to be observed: that the majority should not have the predominant power."

Marcus Tullius Cicero

"Respect for religion must be reestablished. Public debt should be reduced. The arrogance of public officials must be curtailed. Assistance to foreign lands must be stopped or we shall bankrupt ourselves. The people should be forced to work and not depend upon government for subsistence."

Cicero, 60 BC

"...the whole aim of practical politics is to keep the populace alarmed (and hence clamorous to be led to safety) by menacing it with an endless series of hobgoblins, most of them imaginary."

H. L. Mencken
US editor (1880 - 1956)

"In just over 200 years, your country, through freedom and hard work, has changed the world. In agriculture, industry, education, medicine, law, transportation, and on and on.
No country can match America's record in religious freedom, human rights, the importance and dignity of the individual.
We do have our differences. But when we join together in times of crisis, our strength is awesome.
Among all the world's nations, America still stands out front.
You're an American. You're the finest ever and don't you ever, ever forget it."

From an ad of United Technologies

I believe that banking institutions are more dangerous to our liberties than standing armies . . If the American people ever allow private banks to control the issue of their currency, first by inflation, then by deflation, the banks and corporations that will grow up around . . will deprive the people of all property until their children wake-up homeless on the continent their fathers conquered ... The issuing power should be taken from the banks and restored to the people, to whom it properly belongs.

Thomas Jefferson

I cannot undertake to lay my finger on that article of the Constitution which granted a right to Congress of expending, on objects of benevolence, the money of their constituents... If Congress can do whatever in their discretion can be done by money, and will promote the General Welfare, the Government is no longer a limited one, possessing enumerated powers, but an indefinite one, subject to particular exceptions. ... The powers delegated by the proposed Constitution to the federal government are few and defined. Those which are to remain in the State governments are numerous and indefinite. ... There are more instances of the abridgment of the freedom of the people by gradual and silent encroachments of those in power than by violent and sudden usurpations.

James Madison

Those who do not understand our history -- mostly those identified as "liberal" in contemporary vernacular -- assume the words of our Founders are as antiquated as the Declaration and Constitution they created. However, students of history understand that both the threats our Founders confronted at the dawn of our nation, and their advice, have endured to this day.

Author Unknown

We should never despair, our situation before has been unpromising and has changed for the better, so I trust, it will again. If new difficulties arise, we must only put forth new exertions and proportion our efforts to the exigency of the times. ... The name of American, which belongs to you, in your national capacity, must always exalt the just pride of Patriotism, more than any appellation derived from local discriminations. ... It should be the highest ambition of every American to extend his views beyond himself, and to bear in mind that his conduct will not only affect himself, his country, and his immediate posterity; but that its influence may be co-extensive with the world, and stamp political happiness or misery on ages yet unborn. ... The Hand of providence has been so conspicuous in all this, that he must be worse than an infidel that lacks faith, and more than wicked, that has not gratitude enough to acknowledge his obligations. ... [T]he propitious smiles of Heaven, can never be expected on a nation that disregards the eternal rules of order and right, which Heaven itself has ordained.

George Washington

The same prudence which in private life would forbid our paying our own money for unexplained projects, forbids it in the dispensation of the public moneys. ... The multiplication of public offices, increase of expense beyond income, growth and entailment of a public debt, are indications soliciting the employment of the pruning knife. ... We must not let our rulers load us with perpetual debt. ... The principle of spending money to be paid by posterity, under the name of funding, is but swindling futurity on a large scale. ... If we can prevent the government from wasting the labors of the people, under the pretense of taking care of them, they must become happy. ... I think we have more machinery of government than is necessary, too many parasites living on the labor of the industrious. ... The natural progress of things is for liberty to yield and government to gain ground. .... [A] wise and frugal government...shall restrain men from injuring one another, shall leave them otherwise free to regulate their own pursuits of industry and improvement, and shall not take from the mouth of labor the bread it has earned. This is the sum of good government. ... Sometimes it is said that man can not be trusted with government of himself. Can he, then, be trusted with the government of others? Or have we found angels in the forms of kings to govern him? Let history answer this question."

Thomas Jefferson

"I place economy among the first and most important republican virtues, and public debt as the greatest of the dangers to be feared. To preserve our independence, we must not let our rulers load us with perpetual debt."

President Thomas Jefferson 1743-1826

Because socialists reward those who treat money poorly and penalize those who treat money well, the system will never work. True, advocates of wealth redistribution can point to circumstances where it did "work," and where it does "work" from time to time (if only for a limited time). But I can also point to circumstances where the laws of gravity are temporarily suspended, such as when I get on a plane.

But even God will not help me if I just assume because I can fly for a few hours from here to there that I can fly forever. At some point my plane has to come back to the ground. At some point the laws of gravity will resume their authority, and I will realize that my flight and my violation of gravity's laws are coming to an end.

Capitalism is a law established by God, just like gravity. Its foundation is in the 9th Commandment, "Thou shalt not covet." I am never free to desire to take what is my neighbor's. Not his wife. Not his house. Not his lands. Not his possessions. I can trade him for them if I have something he wants more than what he has. (Except his wife, of course…) I can buy them from him if my offer is right. But I cannot steal (or vote) away his property into my account. That is not wealth creation; it is merely re-distribution. God condemns it, and He will not be mocked by those who think that they can make socialism "fly" forever.

Eventually, they will run out of other people's money. And when they do, their plane will come crashing to the ground.

Bill Jenkins

"I hope I shall always possess firmness and virtue enough to maintain what I consider the most enviable of all titles, the character of an honest man."

George Washington

I am not among those who fear the people. They, and not the rich, are our dependence for continued freedom. And to preserve their independence, we must not let our rulers load us with perpetual debt. We must make our election between economy and liberty, or profusion and servitude. If we run into such debts, as that we must be taxed in our meat and in our drink, in our necessities and our comforts, in our labors and our amusements, for our calling and our creeds, as the people of England are, our people, like them, must come to labor sixteen hours in the twenty-four, give the earnings of fifteen of these to the government for their debts and daily expenses; and the sixteenth being insufficient to afford us bread, we must live, as they now do, on oatmeal and potatoes; have no time to think, no means of calling the mismanages to account; but be glad to obtain subsistence by hiring ourselves to rivet their chains on the necks of our fellow suffers. Our land-holders, too, like theirs, retaining indeed the title and stewardship of estates called theirs but held really in trust for the treasury, must wander, like theirs, in foreign countries, and be contented with penury, obscurity, exile, and the glory of the nation. This example reads to us the salutary lesson, that private fortunes are destroyed by public as well as by private extravagances. And this is the tendency of all human governments. A departure from principle in one instance becomes a precedent for the second; that second for a third; and so on, till the bulk of the society is reduced to mere automatons of misery, to have no sensibilities left but for sinning and suffering. Then begins, indeed, the bellum omnium in omnia, which some philosophers observing to be so general in this world, have mistaken for the natural, instead of the abusive state of man. And the fore horse on this frightful team is public debt. Taxation follows that, and in its train wretchedness and oppression.

Thomas Jefferson

Twenty Years Without a Rebellion

God forbid we should ever be twenty years without such a rebellion.

The people cannot be all, and always, well informed. The part which is wrong will be discontented, in proportion to the importance of the facts they misconceive. If they remain quiet under such misconceptions, it is lethargy, the forerunner of death to the public liberty. ...

And what country can preserve its liberties, if it's rulers are not warned from time to time, that this people preserve the spirit of resistance? Let them take arms. The remedy is to set them right as to the facts, pardon and pacify them. What signify a few lives lost in a century or two? The tree of liberty must be refreshed from time to time, with the blood of patriots and tyrants.

It is its natural manure.

Thomas Jefferson

"He does not seem to me to be a free man who does not sometimes do nothing."

Marcus Tullius Cicero

"I have sworn upon the altar of god, eternal hostility against every form of tyranny over the mind of man."

Thomas Jefferson

I say unto you, what does it matter the color of a man's skin if he perjures himself, or if the prosecutor enlists the perjurer, or if the district attorney throws a man to the mob for political gain, and when men of cloth, men of God, take the prime cuts, is that Justice?

I'll tell you what Justice is:
Justice is the Law, and the law is man's feeble attempt to set down the principles of decency. DECENCY.

And decency is not a deal, it isn't an angle, or a hustle, or a contract; Decency is what your grandmother taught you, it's in your bones! Now you go home, go home, and be decent people, be decent.

From the movie "Bonfire of the Vanities"

"Equality under the law is imperative. Equality in everything else is a fantasy."

Norb Svanascini

This morning as I was driving in an expressway under repair at an extremely slow pace, the car in front of me veered on to the exit ramp leaving me in back of a hearse carrying a flag covered coffin. I had never seen in person, a flag covered coffin, and I realized the sorrow for this person that his or her family must have endured. Being a person who has never seen value in war, except to satisfy the ego of someone in power who should have never been put in that position, I wondered why the American people has allowed for hundreds of thousands of their children to be murdered for nothing by these power hungry egomaniacs whose biggest sin is not to heed the warnings of our Founding Fathers "Trade with all countries, make alliances with none". It's amazing to me that the American people still allow this butchery to take place but as the masses say: "We know better"

Norb Svanascini

Power and law are not synonymous. In truth they are frequently in opposition and irreconcilable. There is God's law from which all equitable laws of man emerge and by which men must live if they are not to die in oppression, chaos and despair.

Divorced from God's eternal and immutable law, established before the founding of the suns, man's power is evil no matter the noble words with which it is employed, or the motives used when enforcing it.

Men of good will, mindful therefore of the law laid down by God, will oppose governments whose rule is by men, and if they wish to survive as a nation they will destroy the government which attempts to adjudicate by the whim of venal judges.

Marcus Tullius Cicero
106-43 B.C.

"All the perplexities, confusion and distress in America arise, not from defects in their Constitution or Confederation, not from want of honor or virtue, so much as the downright ignorance of the nature of coin, credit and circulation."

John Adams

A few years back I was in Assisi, Italy one of the most beautiful preserved medieval towns in the world, and I had the pleasure to be taken in a tour by one of the magistrates of that town. In the main "Piazza" or square there were some inscriptions in one of the walls as well as some measurements that were deeply ingrained into the stone. This gentleman told me that these were the "standards" used to measure both lengths as in the stone markings, as well as how weights should be measured.

The reason our financial system is collapsing is because we have ignored our forefathers warnings about a lack of standards in our society, and have abandoned the standards required constitutionally of Gold and Silver. Without "standards" anything goes.

Without a doubt, the Federal Reserve , which is neither "federal" or has any "reserves" is the real Ponzi scheme that dwarfs all other Ponzi schemes put together.

In 1911, coincidentally 2 years before the formation of the Federal Reserve, The London Times printed an editorial regarding America's attempts to make the creation of money a free Constitutional concern: "If this mischievous financial policy, which has its origin in the North American Republic, shall become indurated down to a fixture, then that government will furnish its own money without cost. It will pay off its debts and be without debt. It will have all the money necessary to carry on its commerce. It will become prosperous without precedent in the history of the world. The brains and the wealth of all countries will go to North America. That government MUST be DESTROYED or it will destroy every monarchy on the globe."

And probably, the most important statement ever made about this subject was the following:

If the American people ever allow private banks to control issue of their currency, first by inflation, then by deflation, the banks and the corporations that will grow up around them, will deprive the people of all property until their children wake up homeless on the continent their fathers conquered. The issuing power should be taken from the banks and restored to the people, to whom it properly belongs."--Thomas Jefferson in the debate over his opposition to the Re-charter of the Private Bank Bill (1809).

Norb Svanascini

"Tantum res anxius optat,
Panem et circenses"

(They only want two things, Bread and circuses. Even in Roman times they suffered from the Big Brother and Junk food syndrome!!)
Juvenal

"I am quite sure now that often, very often, in matters concerning religion and politics a man's reasoning powers are not above the monkey's."
Mark Twain in Eruption

Find out just what people will submit to, and you have found out the exact amount of injustice and wrong which will be imposed upon them; and these will continue until they are resisted with either words or blows, or both. The limits of tyrants are prescribed by the endurance of those whom they oppress.

Frederick Douglass

"We will all hang together, or most assuredly we will all hang separately."

Benjamin Franklin

In the 1950's Post magazine had a cartoon with two prehistoric men with bows and arrows. The caption showed one man saying to the other: did you notice that we never had this weather before bows and arrows were invented?

Norb Svanascini

Poor people have traditionally voted the Democratic party since the 1930's. Now, there are more and more poor people. Wealthy people vote traditionally Republican, so it seems to me, if you want to get out of the poor house, maybe you should consider other options.

Norb Svanascini

"Owners of capital will stimulate the working class to buy more and more expensive goods, houses and technology, pushing them to take more and more expensive credit, until their debt becomes unbearable. The unpaid debt will lead to bankruptcy of the banks, which will have to be nationalized. The State will then have to step in to save the banks which will eventually lead to communism."

Karl Marx, 1867

"You cannot strengthen one by weakening another, and you cannot add to the stature of a dwarf by cutting the leg of a giant."

Benjamin Franklin

Corn-pone Opinions by Mark Twain

FIFTY YEARS AGO, when I was a boy of fifteen and helping to inhabit a Missourian village on the banks of the Mississippi, I had a friend whose society was very dear to me because I was forbidden by my mother to partake of it. He was a gay and impudent and satirical and delightful young black man -a slave -who daily preached sermons from the top of his master's woodpile, with me for sole audience. He imitated the pulpit style of the several clergymen of the village, and did it well, and with fine passion and energy. To me he was a wonder. I believed he was the greatest orator in the United States and would some day be heard from. But it did not happen; in the distribution of rewards he was overlooked. It is the way, in this world.

He interrupted his preaching, now and then, to saw a stick of wood; but the sawing was a pretense - he did it with his mouth; exactly imitating the sound the bucksaw makes in shrieking its way through the wood. But it served its purpose; it kept his master from coming out to see how the work was getting along. I listened to the sermons from the open window of a lumber room at the back of the house. One of his texts was this:

"You tell me whar a man gits his corn pone, en I'll tell you what his 'pinions is."

I can never forget it. It was deeply impressed upon me. By my mother. Not upon my memory, but elsewhere. She had slipped in upon me while I was absorbed and not watching. The black philosopher's idea was that a man is not independent, and cannot afford views which might interfere with his bread and butter. If he would prosper, he must train with the majority; in matters of large moment, like politics and religion, he must think and feel with the bulk of his neighbors, or suffer damage in his social standing and in his business prosperities. He must restrict himself to corn-pone opinions -- at least on the surface. He must get his opinions from other people; he must reason out none for himself; he must have no first-hand views.

I think Jerry was right, in the main, but I think he did not go far enough.

1. It was his idea that a man conforms to the majority view of his locality by calculation and intention. This happens, but I think it is not the rule.

2. It was his idea that there is such a thing as a first-hand opinion; an original opinion; an opinion which is coldly reasoned out in a man's head, by a searching analysis of the facts involved, with the heart unconsulted, and the jury room closed against outside influences. It may be that such an opinion has been born somewhere, at some time or other, but I suppose it got away before they could catch it and stuff it and put it in the museum.

I am persuaded that a coldly-thought-out and independent verdict upon a fashion in clothes, or manners, or literature, or politics, or religion, or any other matter that is projected into the field of our notice and interest, is a most rare thing -- if it has indeed ever existed.

A new thing in costume appears -- the flaring hoopskirt, for example

- and the passers-by are shocked, and the irreverent laugh. Six months later everybody is reconciled; the fashion has established itself; it is admired, now, and no one laughs. Public opinion resented it before, public opinion accepts it now, and is happy in it. Why? Was the resentment reasoned out? Was the acceptance reasoned out? No. The instinct that moves to conformity did the work. It is our nature to conform; it is a force which not many can successfully resist. What is its seat? The inborn requirement of self-approval. We all have to bow to that; there are no exceptions. Even the woman who refuses from first to last to wear the hoop skirt comes under that law and is its slave; she could not wear the skirt and have her own approval; and that she must have, she cannot help herself. But as a rule our self-approval has its source in but one place and not elsewhere -- the approval of other people. A person of vast consequences can introduce any kind of novelty in dress and the general world will presently adopt it -- moved to do it, in the first place, by the natural instinct to passively yield to that vague something recognized as authority, and in the second place by the human instinct to train with the multitude and have its approval. An empress introduced the hoopskirt, and we know the result. A nobody introduced the bloomer, and we know the result. If Eve should come again, in her ripe renown, and reintroduce her quaint styles -- well, we know what would happen. And we should be cruelly embarrassed, along at first.

The hoopskirt runs its course and disappears. Nobody reasons about it. One woman abandons the fashion; her neighbor notices this and follows her lead; this influences the next woman; and so on and so on, and presently the skirt has vanished out of the world, no one knows how nor why, nor cares, for that matter. It will come again, by and by and in due course will go again.

Twenty-five years ago, in England, six or eight wine glasses stood grouped by each person's plate at a dinner party, and they were used, not left idle and empty; to-day there are but three or four in the group, and the average guest sparingly uses about two of them. We have not adopted this new fashion yet, but we shall do it presently. We shall not think it out; we shall merely conform, and let it go at that. We get our notions and habits and opinions from outside influences; we do not have to study them out.

Our table manners, and company manners, and street manners change from time to time, but the changes are not reasoned out; we merely notice and conform. We are creatures of outside influences; as a rule we do not think, we only imitate. We cannot invent standards that will stick; what we mistake for standards are only fashions, and perishable. We may continue to admire them, but we drop the use of them. We notice this in literature. Shakespeare is a standard, and fifty years ago we used to write tragedies which we couldn't tell from -- from somebody else's; but we don't do it any more, now. Our prose standard, three quarters of a century ago, was ornate and diffuse; some authority or other changed it in the direction of compactness and simplicity, and conformity followed, without argument. The historical novel starts up suddenly, and sweeps the land. Everybody writes one, and the nation is glad. We had historical novels before; but nobody read them, and the rest of us conformed - without reasoning it out. We are conforming in the other way, now, because it is another case of everybody.

The outside influences are always pouring in upon us, and we are always obeying their orders and accepting their verdicts. The Smiths like the new play; the Joneses go to see it, and they copy the

Smith verdict. Morals, religions, politics, get their following from surrounding influences and atmospheres, almost entirely; not from study, not from thinking. A man must and will have his own approval first of all, in each and every moment and circumstance of his life -- even if he must repent of a self-approved act the moment after its commission, in order to get his self-approval again: but, speaking in general terms, a man's self-approval in the large concerns of life has its source in the approval of the peoples about him, and not in a searching personal examination of the matter. Mohammedans are Mohammedans because they are born and reared among that sect, not because they have thought it out and can furnish sound reasons for being Mohammedans; we know why Catholics are Catholics; why Presbyterians are Presbyterians; why Baptists are Baptists; why Mormons are Mormons; why thieves are thieves; why monarchists are monarchists; why Republicans are Republicans and Democrats, Democrats. We know it is a matter of association and sympathy, not reasoning and examination; that hardly a man in the world has an opinion upon morals, politics, or religion which he got otherwise than through his associations and sympathies. Broadly speaking, there are none but corn-pone opinions. And broadly speaking, corn-pone stands for self-approval. Self-approval is acquired mainly from the approval of other people. The result is conformity. Sometimes conformity has a sordid business interest -- the bread-and-butter interest -- but not in most cases, I think. I think that in the majority of cases it is unconscious and not calculated; that it is born of the human being's natural yearning to stand well with his fellows and have their inspiring approval and praise -- a yearning which is commonly so strong and so insistent that it cannot be effectually resisted, and must have its way. A political emergency brings out the corn-pone opinion in fine force in its two chief varieties -- the pocketbook variety, which has its origin in self-interest, and the bigger variety, the sentimental variety -- the one which can't bear to be outside the pale; can't bear to be in disfavor; can't endure the averted face and the cold shoulder; wants to stand well with his friends, wants to be smiled upon, wants to be welcome, wants to hear the precious words, "He's on the right track!" Uttered, perhaps by an ass, but still an ass of high degree, an ass whose approval is gold and diamonds to a smaller ass, and confers glory and honor and happiness, and membership in the herd. For these gauds many a man will dump his life-long principles into the street, and his conscience along with them. We have seen it happen. In some millions of instances.

Men think they think upon great political questions, and they do; but they think with their party, not independently; they read its literature, but not that of the other side; they arrive at convictions, but they are drawn from a partial view of the matter in hand and are of no particular value. They swarm with their party, they feel with their party, they are happy in their party's approval; and where the party leads they will follow, whether for right and honor, or through blood and dirt and a mush of mutilated morals.

In our late canvass half of the nation passionately believed that in silver lay salvation, the other half as passionately believed that that way lay destruction. Do you believe that a tenth part of the people, on either side, had any rational excuse for having an opinion about the matter at all? I studied that mighty question to the bottom -- came out empty. Half of our people passionately believe in high tariff, the other half believe otherwise. Does this mean study and examination, or only feeling? The latter, I think. I have deeply studied that question, too -- and didn't arrive. We all do no end of feeling, and we mistake it for thinking. And out of it we get an aggregation which we consider a boon. Its name is Public Opinion. It is held in reverence. It settles everything. Some think it the Voice of God.

Mark Twain

In the end, more than freedom, they wanted security. They wanted a comfortable life, and they lost it all-security, comfort, and freedom. When the Athenians finally wanted not to give to society, but for society to give to them, when the freedom they wished for most was freedom from responsibility, then Athens ceased to be free and was never free again.

Edward Gibbon

"Twas ever so, These are times in which a genius would wish to live. It is not in the still calm of life, or the repose of a pacific station, that great characters are formed...Great necessities call out great virtues."

Abigail Adams
letter to John Quincy Adams, 1780

"Evil is making the natural unnatural,
and the unnatural, natural."

Norb Svanascini

Naturally the common people don't want war; neither in Russia, nor in England, nor in America, nor in Germany. That is understood. But after all, it is the leaders of the country who determine policy, and it is always a simple matter to drag the people along, whether it is a democracy, or a fascist dictatorship, or a parliament, or a communist dictatorship.

Voice or no voice, the people can always be brought to the bidding of the leaders. That is easy. All you have to do is to tell them they are being attacked, and denounce the pacifists for lack of patriotism and exposing the country to danger. It works the same in any country.

Reichsmarschall Hermann Goering

"America is like a healthy body and its resistance is threefold: its patriotism, its morality and its spiritual life. If we can undermine these three areas, America will collapse from within."

Josef Stalin

Longshoreman philosopher Eric Hoffer once wrote that all great movements eventually become a business, then degenerate into a racket.

Recommended Movies

Mr Smith Goes to Washington
Legends of the Fall
Lawrence of Arabia
Braveheart
Bridge on the River Kwai
Patton

CHAPTER 3

LOVE

"As soon as forever is through. I'll be over you."

Toto

"Where you used to be, there is a hole in the world, which I find myself constantly walking around in the daytime, and falling in at night. I miss you like hell."

Edna St. Vincent Millay

"Bad as I like ye, it's worse without ye."

Irish Proverb

"Absence diminishes small loves and increases great ones, as the wind blows out the candle and blows up the bonfire."

François de La Rochefoucauld

"To love and win is the best thing. To love and lose, the next best."
William Makepeace Thackeray

"Better to have loved and lost, than to have never loved at all."
St. Augustine

"A mighty pain to love it is, and 'tis a pain that pain to miss; but of all the pains, the greatest pain is to love, but love in vain."
Abraham Crowley

"I have found the paradox, that if you love until it hurts, there can be no more hurt, only more love."
Mother Teresa

I have loved to the point of madness;
That which is called madness,
That which to me,
Is the only sensible way to love.

Françoise Sagan

"I want to do with you what spring does with the cherry trees."

Pablo Neruda

I miss you today, more than I missed you yesterday,
Tomorrow, I'll miss you more than today.

Norb Svanascini

"You'll never know how much I miss you, maybe more; maybe less than
what you miss me, but a whole lot, nevertheless."

Norb Svanascini

Thomas Jefferson was conscious that his love affair was to be short-lived and fragile, yet it was with no especial bitterness that he wrote:
"Deeply practiced in the school of affliction, the human heart knows no joy which I have not lost, no sorrow which I have not drunk."

Thomas Jefferson's letter to Maria Coswell

"Why do I love you? I love you not only for what you are, but for what I am when I am with you. I love you not only for what you have made of yourself, but for what you are making of me. I love you for ignoring the possibilities of the fool in me."

Elizabeth Barret Browning

"A single rose can be my garden... a single friend, my world."

Leo Buscaglia

"Beginning today, treat everyone you meet as if they were going to be dead by midnight. Extend to them all the care, kindness, and understanding you can muster, and do it with no thought of any reward. Your life will never be the same again."

Og Mandino

"I truly want to possess unconditional love. I know the value of it. I want to possess all of the virtues, like forgiveness, compassion, integrity and sundry. I very easily forgive people, even when they are incapable of forgiving me. When people meet and that special chemistry goes off between them, it makes them feel free. It is liberating. That is one of the chief qualities of love that makes it such a desirable experience. What people do, all too soon, is to then get attached to the other person and seek to control them and regulate their behavior and the liberty and freedom goes away."

Author Unknown

"On this Valentine's Day, may all the people that are truly loved without any reservations by someone they no longer love, be as happy as their old love was when they were a pair."

Norb Svanascini

"True love has no other interest or requirements, it has no beauty, it has no jewels, it has no money, in short, there are no 'deals' in true love."

Norb Svanascini

"Love is not blind - it sees more, not less. But because it sees more, it is willing to see less."

Julius Gordon

"A mother is only as happy as her saddest child."

Norb Svanascini

Angrily I searched for her,
Happily I found her,
As usual, I adored her.

Norb Svanascini

"Love is life. And if you miss love, you miss life."

Leo Buscaglia

"There is always some madness in love. But there is also always some reason in madness."

Friedrich Nietzsche

"The meeting of two personalities is like the contact of two chemical substances: if there is any reaction, both are transformed."

Carl Jung

A brief candle; both ends burning
An endless mile; a bus wheel turning
A friend to share the lonesome times
A handshake and a sip of wine
So say it loud and let it ring
We are all a part of everything
The future, present and the past
Fly on proud bird
You're free at last.

Charlie Daniels

"Him that I love, I wish to be free - even from me."
Anne Morrow Lindbergh

Now I will make up an exact statement, and please keep it in mind however dumb I might be, because it is at all times true.

1. I want to keep you and I want not to ruin your life. Compared to these two, all other things in life are trivial to me. Don't doubt this.
2. I want to accomplish, during my life, a good deal more work in philosophy.
3. I want to write things on religion and morals and popular philosophy. I could do this even if I were discredited, because I could publish anonymously.
4. I like teaching, but that is inessential. I have put these four in order of importance, the most important first. Whatever may be involved in our holding to each other, the harm to me will be less than if we parted. I believe seriously that the spring of life would be broken in me if we parted. If I have you, there are other goods that might be added; if I don't have you, there are no other goods. I have never imagined such love. I have had the feeling too that I ought to keep it back from you so as not to interfere with your freedom-but I can't. With you there is life and peace and joy and all good things away from you there is turmoil and anguish and blank despair

Bertrand Russel

"There is no remedy for love but to love more."

Henry David Thoreau

If I had a flower for every time I think of you… I could walk forever in my garden."

Author Unknown

Sometimes we forget anniversaries.
Sometimes we ignore them.
If we forget, it's excusable
If we ignore, someone is waiting.
Sometimes we acknowledge
sometimes we don't
but even if one remembers
the anniversary exists

Norb Svanascini

You have been my friend. That in itself is a tremendous thing. I wove my webs for you because I liked you. After all, what's a life, anyway? We're born, we live a little while, we die. A spider's life can't help being something of a mess, with all this trapping and eating flies. By helping you, perhaps I was trying to lift up my life a trifle. Heaven knows anyone's life can stand a little of that.

Charlotte
"Charlotte's Web" by E.B. White

"Please allow me to wipe the slate clean. Age has no reality except in the physical world. The essence of a human being is resistant to the passage of time. Our inner lives are eternal, which is to say that our spirits remain as youthful and vigorous as when we are in full bloom. Think of love as a state of grace, not as a mean to anything, but the Alpha and Omega. An end in itself."

Gabriel García Márquez
From the movie "Love in the Time of Cholera"

"All love that has not friendship for its base,
Is like a mansion built upon the sand."

Ella Wheeler Wilcox

"A woman's lips, warmth, snow, happiness."

Norb Svanascini

"Woman, Gibraltar, the petals of a rose."

Norb Svanascini

"A woman, like a diamond, sparkles when admired."

Norb Svanascini

The Devoted Son

Years ago, there was a very wealthy man who, with his devoted young son, shared a passion for art collecting. Together they traveled around the world, adding only the finest treasures to their collection. Priceless works by Picasso, Van Gogh, Monet and many others adorned the walls of their family estate. The widowed elderly man looked on with satisfaction as his only child became an experienced art collector. The son's trained eye and sharp business mind caused his father to beam with pride as they dealt with art collectors around the world.

As winter approached, war engulfed their nation, and the young man left to serve his country. After only a few short weeks, the elderly man received a telegram that his beloved son was missing in action. The art collector anxiously awaited more news, fearing he would never see his son again. Within days, his fears were confirmed. The young man had died while rushing a fellow soldier to a medic. Distraught and lonely, the old man faced the upcoming Christmas holidays with anguish and sadness. The joy of the season -- a season he and his son had so looked forward to in the past -- would visit his house no longer. On Christmas morning, a knock on the door awakened the depressed old man. As he walked to the door, the masterpieces of art on the walls only reminded him that his son was not coming home. He opened the door and was greeted by a soldier with a large package in his hand.

The soldier introduced himself to the old man, saying, "I was a friend of your son. I was the one he was rescuing when he died. May I come in for a few moments? I have something to show you."

As the two began to talk, the soldier told of how the man's son had told everyone of his – and his father's -- love of fine art work. "I'm also an artist," said the soldier, "and I want to give you this." As the old man began to unwrap the package, paper gave way to reveal a portrait of the man's son. Though the world would never consider it a work of genius, the painting featured the young man's face in striking detail.

Overcome with emotion, the old man thanked the soldier, promising to hang the portrait above the fireplace. A few hours later, after the soldier had departed, the old man set about his task. True to his word, the painting went above the fireplace, pushing aside thousands of dollars worth of paintings. And then the old man sat in his chair and spent Christmas gazing at the gift he had been given. During the days and weeks that followed, the man learned that his son had rescued dozens of wounded soldiers before a bullet stilled his caring heart. As the stories of his son's gallantry continued to reach him, fatherly pride and satisfaction began to ease his grief, as he realized that, although his son was no longer with him, the boy's life would live on because of those he had touched.

The painting of his son soon became his most prized possession, far eclipsing any interest in the priceless pieces for which museums around the world clamored. He told his neighbors it was the greatest gift he had ever received. The following spring, the old man became ill and passed away. The art world was in anticipation, since, with the old man's passing and his only son dead, those paintings would be sold at auction. According to the will of the old man, all of the art works would be auctioned on Christmas Day, the way he had received his greatest gift.

The day finally arrived, and art collectors from around the world gathered to bid on some of the world's most spectacular paintings. Dreams could be fulfilled this day; greatness could be achieved as some could say," I have the greatest collection."

The auction began with a painting that was not on any museum list. It was the painting of the old man's son. The auctioneer asked for an opening bid, but the room was silent.

"Who will open the bidding with $100?" he asked. Moments passed as no one spoke. From the back of the room came, "Who cares about that painting? It's just a picture of his son. Let's forget it and get on to the good ones." More voices echoed in agreement. "No, we have to sell this one first," replied the auctioneer. "Now who will take the son?"

Finally, a friend of the old man spoke. "Will you take $10 for the painting? That's all I have."

"Will anyone go higher?" called the auctioneer. After more silence he said, "Going once, going twice ... gone!" The gavel fell. Cheers filled the room and someone shouted, "Now we can get on with it and bid on these treasures!"

The auctioneer looked at the audience and announced that the auction was over. Stunned disbelief quieted the room. Then someone spoke up and asked, "What do you mean it's over? We didn't come here for a portrait of some old man's son! What about all of the other paintings? There are millions of dollars worth of art work here. We demand an explanation!"

The auctioneer replied, "It's very simple. According to the will of the father, whoever takes the son gets it all."

Just as the art collectors discovered on that day, the message is still the same. The love of the father ... a father whose son gave his life for others ... and because of that father's love ... whoever takes the son gets it all.

Author Unknown

RECOMMENDED MOVIES

Casablanca
Cinema Paradiso
Cyrano de Bergerac (Jose Ferrer)
Fanny (Leslie Caron)
Back Street (Charles Boyer)
From the Terrace
Ten North Frederick
Indecent Proposal
The Notebook
An Affair to Remember
Somewhere in Time

CHAPTER 4

BUSINESS

"The chief business of the American people is business. They are profoundly concerned with producing, buying, selling, investing and prospering in the world."

Calvin Coolidge

"One machine can do the work of fifty ordinary men.
No machine can do the work of an extraordinary man."

Elbert Hubbard

"Strive for perfection in everything.
take the best that exists and make it better.
If it doesn't exist, create it.
Accept nothing nearly right or good enough."

Sir Henry Royce
Co-founder of Rolls Royce

This was the hardest thing to learn when I was 19. When we first started doing Penn & Teller shows, I thought that if you had a contract, it was enforced. I thought there were the contract police so you'd sign a contract that says you're going to give me a million dollars, and if you don't have a million dollars, someone will step in and give me my million anyway. Right.

That's one of the hardest lessons for a guy like me who has no interest in business but now runs a multimillion-dollar enterprise. A contract is not much of a legal document. It's just an agreement that two people who trust each other have made. You can't enter into a contract with anyone that you wouldn't make a handshake deal with, because everything comes down to a handshake deal. The more experience I got in showbiz, the less I read the contracts. Now I don't bother. If I can't make the deal in a phone call, and have them understand it, then it's not a worthwhile deal. You're making a deal with the people, not with the contract. That's a mistake that people make a lot: "We've got it in writing now." The contract is clarification, but it's not enforcement.

Penn Jillette
Magician, author, & producer

"If people knew how hard I had to work to gain my mastery, it would not so seem wonderful at all."

Michelangelo

"Genius is one percent inspiration, and ninety-nine percent perspiration."
Thomas Edison

"Doing well is the result of doing good. That's what capitalism is all about."

Ralph Waldo Emerson

"The three great essentials to achieving anything worthwhile are; first, hard work, second, stick-to-it-iveness, and third, common sense."
Thomas Edison

Traveling through Europe, It's interesting how every country is proud of the works of art and architectural achievements that their heritage holds. In Austria we visited a monastery in a city called Melk.

This magnificent castle, carefully named a monastery, is world renowned by its wealth in gold and opulence, and of course was built by the people preaching that their purpose in life, was to help the poor. We were also told that one wing of this monastery was reserved for princess Maria Theresa of Austria when she visited the monastery as she traveled with her 300 +assistants that accompanied her to keep her hair in good shape as well as to cater to her other needs at all times.

It dawned on me, why are the people of these countries proud to talk about these people that basically contributed nothing to the betterment of mankind, and conversely abused and stole from the same people they were living off, under the pretense that they were protecting them from the hardships of this life or the next.

I wondered as an American, for a very short moment I must say, what America can show to the world; and I realized that America shows itself every moment of the day to almost every human on earth. From the time that a European doesn't have to light a candle, he should thank an American. When an Asian wants to listen to music without having to go to a designated place with musicians playing, he can play his phonograph or listen to his I-pod or play his records, he can thank an American, and when someone anyplace in the world gets in his car, he can thank an American, and when he goes home in the middle of summer and feels cool air coming from an air conditioning system, he can thank an American, and so on and so on.

You see, in about 200 years, America built and created things for all men, not just some men; it's just that simple.

You don't have to travel far to see America, just turn the light switch on.

Norb Svanascini

"If you don't have any idea of what you're talking about, anything is possible."

Norb Svanascini

Why are some people more successful than others? Why do some people make more money, live happier lives and accomplish much more in the same number of years than the great majority?

I started out in life with few advantages. I did not graduate from high school. I worked at menial jobs. I had limited education, limited skills and a limited future.

And then I began asking, "Why are some people more successful than others?" This question changed my life.

Over the years, I have read thousands of books and articles on the subjects of success and achievement. It seems that the reasons for these accomplishments have been discussed and written about for more than two thousand years, in every conceivable way. One quality that most philosophers, teachers and experts agree on is the importance of self-discipline. As Al Tomsik summarized it years ago, "Success is tons of discipline."

Some years ago, I attended a conference in Washington. It was the lunch break and I was eating at a nearby food fair. The area was crowded and I sat down at the last open table by myself, even though it was a table for four.

A few minutes later, an older gentleman and a younger woman who was his assistant came along carrying trays of food, obviously looking for a place to sit.

With plenty of room at my table, I immediately arose and invited the older gentleman to join me. He was hesitant, but I insisted.

Finally, thanking me as he sat down, we began to chat over lunch. It turned out that his name was Kop Kopmeyer. As it happened, I immediately knew who he was. He was a legend in the field of success and achievement. Kop Kopmeyer had written four large books, each of which contained 250 success principles that he had derived from more than fifty years of research and study. I had read all four books from cover to cover, more than once.

After we had chatted for awhile, I asked him the question that many people in this situation would ask, "Of all the one thousand success principles that you have discovered, which do you think is the most important?"

He smiled at me with a twinkle in his eye, as if he had been asked this question many times, and replied, without hesitating, "The most important success principle of all was stated by Thomas Huxley many years ago. He said, 'Do what you should do, when you should do it, whether you feel like it or not.'"

He went on to say, "There are 999 other success principles that I have found in my reading and experience, but without self-discipline, none of them work."

Self-discipline is the key to personal greatness. It is the magic quality that opens all doors for you, and makes everything else possible. With self-discipline, the average person can rise as far and as fast as his talents and intelligence can take him. But without self-discipline, a person with every blessing of background, education and opportunity will seldom rise above mediocrity.

From "The Power of Discipline" by Brian Tracy

Prosperity is something the businessmen created for politicians to take credit for

Ralph Waldo Emerson

One of the most amazing things I've observed is that most people would not get themselves into a financial mess if they would just multiply.

I've always traveled; many times to Europe and people asked : how do you do it?

I say : I multipy--for example, you smoke, that's $5 a day multiplied by 365 days, equals $1,825 which will pay for a week in Europe. You drink whatever at $20 a week and its $1040 a year. Anything that costs $40 a month is $480 a year and so on.

Get in the habit of multiplying and soon you'll discover the amount of money you can re-direct with things you might be happier with.

Norb Svanascini

"It ought to be remembered that there is nothing more difficult to take in hand, more perilous to conduct, or more uncertain in its success, than to take the lead in the introduction of a new order of things. Because the innovator has for enemies all those who have done well under the old conditions, and lukewarm defenders among those who may do well under the new."

Machiavelli
The Prince

People who run with the crowd get lost in the crowd. So stand up for what you believe, even if you're the only one who believes it. At meetings, be the first to speak out, rather than the last to agree. Have the guts to admit when you're wrong, and the grace not to swagger when you're right; yes there might be comfort in numbers, but people often rise to great heights the same way kites do, against the wind, not with it.

Ad by Meldrum & Fewsmith
an advertising agency out of Cleveland, Ohio

"Impossible is a word to be found only in the dictionary of fools."

Napoleon Bonaparte

"A man without enthusiasm is like an automobile without gasoline."

Napoleon Hill

"Keep away from people who try to belittle your ambitions. Small people always do that, but the really great make you feel that you, too, can become great."

Mark Twain

"If you accomplish your goals, but you need your youth to make them right, let your children be your youth, and they will make it right for you."

Mike Svanascini
(at 13 years of age)

"The highest reward for a man's toil is not what he gets for it, but what he becomes by it."

John Ruskin

It has been said that salesmen are a big problem to their bosses, their wives, conservative credit managers, to hotels, and sometimes to each other.

They live in hotels, on trains, airplanes, in automobiles, buses, and cabs. They eat all kinds of food, drink all kinds of liquids —good and bad; and sleep before, during and after business.

In many ways, they are a tribute unto themselves. They draw and spend more money with less effort and get smaller value than any other civilized group in business. They come at the most inopportune time, under the slightest pretext, stay longer under more opposition, ask more personal questions, make more comments, put up with more inconveniences and take more for granted, under greater resistance, than any other group or body, including standing armies.

They make more noise and mistakes, correct more errors, cause more divorces, explain more discrepancies, bear more grievances, pacify more belligerents, and lose more time under high pressure (without losing their temper) than any class we know, including their ministers. They introduce more new goods, start more new businesses and write more debits and credits in our ledgers than any other group in America.

And when buyers find themselves in a tight spot they usually pick out, from one of their salesmen friends, one of several in whom they have total confidence for counsel and advice, and they get it---Clean and Straight.

Author Unknown

"The test of management is the ability to make the best decision between two or more questionable decisions."

Norb Svanascini

"Things might come to those to wait, but only the things by those who hustle."

Abraham Lincoln

"Hell, there are no rules here - we're trying to accomplish something."

Thomas Edison

Do You Remember Who Gave You Your First Break?

Someone saw something in you once. That's partly why you are where you are today. It could have been a thoughtful parent, a perceptive teacher, a demanding drill sergeant, an appreciative employer, or just a friend who dug down in his pocket and came up with a few bucks. Whoever it was, had the kindness and the foresight to bet on your future. Those are two beautiful qualities that separate the human being from the orangutan. In the next 24 hours, take 10 minutes to write a grateful note to the person who helped you. You'll keep a wonderful friendship alive. Matter a fact, take another 10 minutes to give someone else a break. Who knows? Someday you might get a nice letter. It could be one of the most gratifying messages you ever read.

This was an ad published in the Wall Street Journal by United Technologies

"Render more and better than that which you are paid and sooner or later you'll receive compound interest from your investment. It is inevitable that every seed of service you sow will multiply and come back to you in overwhelming abundance."

Napoleon Hill

"If you're in control, you're going too slow."

Mario Andretti

THE CHAIR

And it came to pass that I was looking for a chair last Christmas. I wanted to buy my wife a small telephone chair. I wanted it to be something special; a conversation piece; something that would delight her. It was for the telephone in the butler's pantry which she uses most during the day for her shopping and her long visits with her friends. As it was, she had to drag a chair from the kitchen or dining room.

So, I looked for the right chair, and I found it. I was delighted, and I knew my wife would be. Yes, it could be delivered in plenty of time for Christmas; I was assured by the personable young salesman. There was only one thing: I naturally did not want my wife to know she was getting a telephone chair until we opened our presents on Christmas morning. "Will you gift wrap it?" I asked.

The salesman shook his head. "Sorry, we can't wrap it. It will be delivered as you see it know." But this would take all the fun out of it!

Just put it in an old cardboard box, and I'll gift wrap it myself. The salesman could not do it as it was company policy that this can't be done. The chair would be delivered as is, and Santa Claus would just have to like it, or lump it. In the meantime, The salesman had completed the order and handed it to me for my signature. I shook my head. Sorry, but I will try to find a store with a staff willing to do a little bit more for the customer than just to write up an order. I left.

At another very good store, I found another chair that would fill the bill; but the aging, unhappy salesman gave me the same story, no gift wrapping, no box.

Next, I chose the biggest store in town. After two more hours of searching, I found still another chair; and though a little more expensive than the first two, it was an exact reproduction of a famous chair that Napoleon's Josephine used to sit upon.

I'll take it, I said. Then I paused and silently prayed that I would not again have to continue my odyssey. "Can you gift wrap it for me?" We sure can, he said. We'll find a box that will fit it, wrap it real nice, and your wife will be surprised on Christmas morning." Thank you, I said. You have no idea how much I appreciate that, and you know, since you've been so helpful about it, I saw that Chaise lounge over there.

Well that is the story of the chair, and it's the story of why people change their buying habits; It is also the reason the biggest store in town is the biggest, and why you would recognize the name if I mentioned it. You might not recognize the name of the other two stores. I won't in the future. They refused me when I needed their help. They didn't earn my money or my future patronage, and so, they will get neither. As it is with living creatures, business is a matter of natural selection; the survival of the fittest.

Earl Nightingale

"He who has begun, has the work half done."

Horace

"Start by doing what's necessary, then what's possible, and suddenly you are doing the impossible."

St. Francis of Assisi

110 MINUTE EXPLANATION ON HOW ECONOMIES WORK

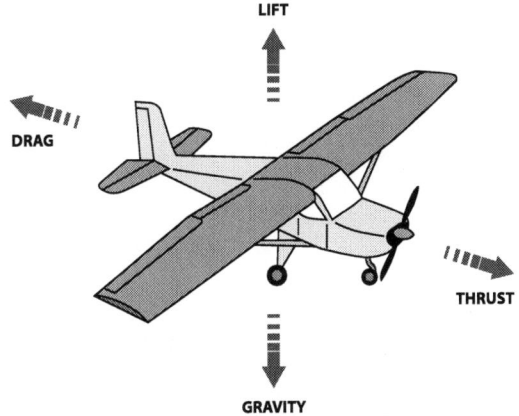

As a young man who loved flying both model and real airplanes, and having to learn the forces that act upon a plane in flight, while at the same time always being enamored with the economy and how it worked, it came to me that the similarities were obvious, and if we replace "Gravity" with acts of God (things you cannot control, i.e. weather, death, sickness) "Drag" (things we can control but impose on the economy, i.e. politics), "Thrust" with Business and Industry, "Lift" with the corresponding result of these forces; the obvious parallel is self explanatory

Norb Svanascini

ROMANS AND THE SPACE SHUTTLE

Railroad tracks.

Be sure to read the final paragraph; your understanding of it will depend on the earlier part of the content.

The US standard railroad gauge (distance between the rails) is 4 feet, 8.5 inches. That's an exceedingly odd number.

Why was that gauge used? Because that's the way they built them in England, and English expatriates built the US railroads.

Why did the English build them like that? Because the first rail lines were built by the same people who built the pre-railroad tramways, and that's the gauge they used.

Why did 'they' use that gauge then? Because the people who built the tramways used the same jigs and tools that they used for building wagons, which used that wheel spacing.

Why did the wagons have that particular odd wheel spacing? Well, if they tried to use any other spacing, the wagon wheels would break on some of the old, long distance roads in England, because that's the spacing of the wheel ruts.

So who built those old rutted roads? Imperial Rome built the first long distance roads in Europe (and England) for their legions. The roads have been used ever since.

And the ruts in the roads? Roman war chariots formed the initial ruts, which everyone else had to match for fear of destroying their wagon wheels. Since the chariots were made for Imperial Rome, they were all alike in the matter of wheel spacing. Therefore the United States standard railroad gauge of 4 feet, 8.5 inches is derived from the original specifications for an Imperial Roman war chariot. Bureaucracies live forever.

So the next time you are handed a Specification/Procedure/ Process and wonder 'What horse's ass came up with it?' You may be exactly right. Imperial Roman army chariots were made just wide enough to accommodate the rear ends of two war horses. (Two horses' asses.) Now, the twist to the story:

When you see a Space Shuttle sitting on its launch pad, there are two big booster rockets attached to the sides of the main fuel tank. These are solid rocket boosters, or SRB's. The SRB's are made by Thiokol at their factory in Utah. The engineers who designed the SRB's would have preferred to make them a bit fatter, but the SRB's had to be shipped by train from the factory to the launch site. The railroad line from the factory happens to run through a tunnel in the mountains, and the SRB's had to fit through that tunnel. The tunnel is slightly wider than the railroad track, and the railroad track, as you now know, is about as wide as two horses' asses.

So, a major Space Shuttle design feature of what is arguably the world's most advanced transportation system was determined over two thousand years ago by the width of a horse's ass. And you thought being a horse's ass wasn't important? Ancient horse's asses control almost everything...and...CURRENT Horses Asses are controlling everything else.

Author Unknown

RECOMMENDED MOVIES

The Godfather
The Thomas Crown Affair (Steve McQueen)
The Fountainhead
Once Upon A Time In America

CHAPTER 5

EDUCATION

"Education is what remains after one has forgotten what one has learned in school."

Albert Einstein

"The aim of education should be to teach a child to think, not what to think."

John Dewey

"Nothing in this world can take the place of persistence. Talent will not: nothing is more common than unsuccessful men with talent. Genius will not; unrewarded genius is almost a proverb. Education will not: the world is full of educated derelicts. Persistence and determination alone are omnipotent."

Calvin Coolidge

"If I am walking with two other men, each of them will serve as my teacher. I will pick out the good points of the one and imitate them, and the bad points of the other and correct them in myself."

Confucius

TEACHER'S JOB

There's only one job for a teacher, and that is to inspire the child to want to learn, as when that learning spark ignites, there is no need to teach anything else. In every child there is a hidden lock, which when opened, the desire to learn kicks in. The real teacher holds the key to that lock, as he/she knows that once it's opened, teaching becomes nothing else but a support system.

Norb Svanascini

"I prefer the company of peasants because they have not been educated sufficiently to reason incorrectly."

Michel de Montaigne

"When education becomes a tool for popular and accepted social thought patterns to be taught, it becomes indoctrination.
The result: making totally worthless societies."

Norb Svanascini

"Te art of healing comes from nature, not from the physician. Therefore the physician must start from nature, with an open mind."

Paracelsus

"Only the wisest and stupidest of men never change."

Confucius

"To enjoy good health, to bring true happiness to one's family, to bring peace to all, one must first discipline and control one's own mind. If a man can control his mind he can find the way to Enlightenment, and all wisdom and virtue will naturally come to him."

Buddha

"Education should be only devoted to the expansion of the ability to think. When the educational system teaches theories that are erroneous as fact, and pass out degrees according to the student's ability to agree and learn these theories, and jobs are given to people who learned those theories so they can practice them in everyday life as facts, the inevitability of the result is mathematic in nature."

Norb Svanascini

"Good manners will open doors that the best education cannot."

Clarence Thomas

In Academia, where everything is explained rationally, Murphy's law doesn't exist.

Norb Svanascini

Why is it that mankind cannot accept political failures as fact, but it can respect scientific failures as fact. Educators would be laughed out of College and University campuses if they were in the scientific fields and stood in front of their audience and preached that the electric theories as we know them are all wrong, and we must ignore the light bulb and electric motors, etc., as flukes, and must go back to candlelight and horse power until we find the "true electricity" that is bound to come by discussion. Why is it then that Educators today not only ignore the fruits of American ideals which produced the greatest social advancements in the history of mankind, but for the past 6 or seven decades we have filled our Colleges and Universities with so called educators who want to discard these advancements as flukes and only concentrate on the things that are still not perfect; and to make matters more ridiculous, their so called solutions are the over and over **PROVEN** methods that do not work.

Is the inevitability of stupidity inevitable in human history?

Norb Svanascini

Belief in teachers and masters outside of our own awareness is a confession of ignorance and slavery. Leaning on these mirages will eventually result in a fall to the ground.

Man's weakness for leaders, and his worship of idols makes him an easy mark for schools, teachers, governments, masters, clergy, presidents, authors, and outside authority figures of all kinds. Good will eventually come of this to everyone as they will discover after years of subjection to these "outside" agents, of waiting lazily for some writer, or teacher to show them the way, that what they've been looking for can't be found in another. That there is only one master, their own awareness, the unique God within themselves. Stop looking for the teacher to come, lean on your own version of truth that comes from the center of yourself. This is the only authentic savior you will ever experience.

Instead of developing the imagination of man, our educational system stifles it by attempting to put in our minds the wisdom that we seek. It forces us to memorize a number of text books, which all too soon are disproved by later text books. Education and first person spirituality is not accomplished by putting something into man; its purpose is to draw out of us the wisdom latent within us, the first person experience of ourselves as God. This "peep show" culture of ours isolates us from the assumption that we have the knowledge and truth within ourselves and we go running everywhere to find it, in books, churches, temples, rituals, observances, best sellers, and talk show hosts.

There is a divine conspiracy of the entire universe to help each of us find, develop, and express our own truth. Each of us individually is as qualified as anyone ever was or ever will be, to unravel the mysteries of life. This conspiracy waits patiently for you the subject, to step forward and identify yourself as the commander, to stop laying yourself before servants, and accepting the second hand experiences of others as the spiritual truth and fire of your own being. There is only one everlasting Lord and Master; your awareness of being. This is what is peeling back the layers of reality, moving you however haltingly, back to the recollection of who and what you are as God. Enjoy writers and entertainers but don't substitute their synthesis of truth and reality for your own. Seek your own counsel as much as you can. Dependence on anyone or anything else will eventually result in disappointment and this may be, as it always was.

Author Unknown

"A drop of ink may make a million think."

Lord Byron

Children should be educated and instructed in the principles of freedom. ... If we suffer [the minds of young people] to grovel and creep in infancy, they will grovel all their lives. ... The foundation of national morality must be laid in private families... How is it possible that Children can have any just Sense of the sacred Obligations of Morality or Religion if, from their earliest Infancy, they learn their Mothers live in habitual Infidelity to their fathers, and their fathers in as constant Infidelity to their Mothers? ... We have no government armed with power capable of contending with human passions unbridled by morality and religion. Avarice, ambition, revenge, or gallantry, would break the strongest cords of our Constitution as a whale goes through a net. Our Constitution was made only for a moral and religious people. It is wholly inadequate to the government of any other. ... The only foundation of a free Constitution, is pure Virtue, and if this cannot be inspired into our People ... they may change their Rulers, and the forms of Government, but they will not obtain a lasting Liberty. ... A Constitution of Government once changed from Freedom, can never be restored. Liberty, once lost, is lost forever.

John Adams

The Man in the Glass

If you're starting to feel that you're cock of the walk
'cause you've just gotten thrown a bouquet,
Then you really should go to a mirror and look
to find out what THAT man has to say.
For it isn't your father or mother or wife
on whose judgement you'll fail or you'll pass--
For the fellow whose verdict counts most in your life
is the one staring back from the glass.
Now some people might think you're the king who has come,
and they'll sing out your praise to the sky;
but the man in the glass says you're only a bum
if you can't look at him straight in the eye.
He's the fellow to please-never mind all the rest-
For he's with you, you see, till the end;

And you'll know that you've passed your most difficult test
if the guy in the glass is your friend.
You may fool the whole world throughout all of your years,
and great accolades when you pass;
but your final reward will be the heartache and tears
if you cheated the man in the glass.

Author Unknown

RECOMMENDED MOVIES

Dead Poets Society
Goodbye Mr. Chips
Boys Town

CHAPTER 6

RELIGION

When Billy Graham was 92-years-old with Parkinson's disease, in January 2000, leaders in Charlotte, North Carolina, invited him, their favorite son, to a luncheon in his honor. Billy initially hesitated to accept the invitation because he struggles with Parkinson's disease but the Charlotte leaders said, 'We don't expect a major address. Just come and let us honor you.' So he agreed. After wonderful things were said about him, Dr. Graham stepped to the rostrum, looked at the crowd, and said, "I'm reminded today of Albert Einstein, the great physicist who this month has been honored by Time magazine as the Man of the Century. Einstein was once traveling from Princeton on a train when the conductor came down the aisle, punching the tickets of every passenger. When he came to Einstein, Einstein reached in his vest pocket. He couldn't find his ticket, so he reached in his trouser pockets. It wasn't there. He looked in his briefcase but couldn't find it. Then he looked in the seat beside him. He still couldn't find it. "The conductor said, 'Dr. Einstein, I know who you are. We all know who you are. I'm sure you bought a ticket. Don't worry about it.' "Einstein nodded appreciatively.

The conductor continued down the aisle punching tickets. As he was ready to move to the next car, he turned around and saw the great physicist down on his hands and knees looking under his seat for his ticket. "The conductor rushed back and said, 'Dr. Einstein, Dr. Einstein, don't worry, I know who you are; no problem. You don't need a ticket. I'm sure you bought one.' Einstein looked at him and said, 'Young man, I too, know who I am. What I don't know is where I'm going." Having said that Billy Graham continued, "See the suit I'm wearing? It's a brand new suit. My children, and my grandchildren are telling me I've gotten a little slovenly in my old age. I used to be a bit more fastidious. So I went out and bought a new suit for this luncheon and one more occasion. You know what that occasion is? This is the suit in which I'll be buried. But when you hear I'm dead, I don't want you to immediately remember the suit I'm wearing. I want you to remember this: I not only know who I am. I also know where I'm going." May your troubles be less, your blessings more, and may nothing but happiness, come through your door. "Life without God is like an unsharpened pencil - it has no point."
Amen & Peace My Friends.

Norb Svanascini

Upon entering the gates of Heaven, St. Peter asked: "Where are your scars?"

The man responded: "What scars?"

St. Peter responded: "You found nothing to fight for while you were on earth?"

"Let us not listen to those who think we ought to be angry with our enemies, and who believe this to be great and manly. Nothing is so praiseworthy, nothing so clearly shows a great and noble soul, as clemency and readiness to forgive."

Marcus Tullius Cicero

"If you are depressed you are living in the past.
If you are anxious you are living in the future.
If you are at peace you are living in the present."

Lao Tzu

Our Creator and Redeemer... and do we THINK about it??? God's accuracy may be observed in the hatching of eggs...

For example:
- The eggs of the potato bug hatch in 7 days;
- Those of the canary in 14 days;
- Those of the barnyard hen in 21 days;
- The eggs of ducks and geese hatch in 28 days;
- Those of the mallard in 35 days;
- The eggs of the parrot and the ostrich hatch in 42 days.

(Notice, they are all divisible by seven, the number of days in a week!)

God's wisdom is seen in the making of an elephant. The four legs of this great beast all bend forward in the same direction. No other quadruped is so made. God planned that this animal would have a huge body, too large to live on two legs. For this reason He gave it four fulcrums so that it can rise from the ground easily.

The horse rises from the ground on its two front legs first. A cow rises from the ground with its two hind legs first. How wise the Lord is in all His works of creation!

God's wisdom is revealed in His arrangement of sections and segments, as well as in the number of grains.

- Each watermelon has an even number of stripes on the rind.
- Each orange has an even number of segments.
- Each ear of corn has an even number of rows.
- Each stalk of wheat has an even number of grains.
- Every bunch of bananas has on its lowest row an even number of bananas, and each row decreases by one, so that one row has an even number and the next row an odd number.
- The waves of the sea roll in on shore twenty-six to the minute in all kinds of weather.

All grains are found in even numbers on the stalks, and the Lord specified thirty fold, sixty fold, and a hundred fold, all even numbers.

God has caused the flowers to blossom at certain specified times during the day. Linnaeus, the great botanist, once said that if he had a conservatory containing the right kind of soil, moisture and temperature, he could tell the time of day or night by the flowers that were open and those that were closed!

The lives of each of you may be ordered by the Lord in a beautiful way for His glory, if you will only entrust Him with your life.

If you try to regulate your own life, it will only be a mess and a failure. Only the One Who made the brain and the heart can successfully guide them to a profitable end.

Author Unknown

After living a great life and meeting thousands of people both good and bad, it struck me that in talking with people that I admired, but were raised with different religious ideas, that all of them were sincere about their beliefs and had a deep respect for their religion. It also occurred to me that unless there were multi-possible occurrences that occur with religious beliefs, most of these ideas were wrong, as there is probably one answer, and the probability is that none of the religions practiced have it 100% correct; so it came to me that the problem with mankind is not with their beliefs, but with their inability to accept the possibility that they could be wrong.

Norb Svanascini

"Faith consists in believing when it is beyond the power of reason to believe."

Voltaire

My daughter had an heiress in her elementary school class. The two were discussing their various bedtime, and the heiress said that every evening at 10 o'clock, she went to the small refrigerator in her room, and took out the usual snack: fresh berries and organic yogurt with honey. My daughter asked: "Who puts it there?" The heiress paused for a while, and said, "I don't know." The great fault of my generation is not ingratitude, but incomprehension. SOMEONE must make the money.

SOMEONE must provide the goods and services we all enjoy.

"The Secret Knowledge:
On the Dismantling of American Culture" by David Mamet

ORGANIZED RELIGIONS EXPLAINED

Where we stopped, grass spread around us like an emerald pond cupped in mountains. Sunset flamed from crimson clouds. Switzerland, I thought at once, we've landed on a Swiss postcard. Away down in the valley was a sweep of trees, sudden houses, high peaked roofs, a church steeple. There was a cart on the village road, pulled not by tractor or horse but by some kind of cow.

I saw no one nearby, not a path, not a goat-trail. Just this lake of grass, sprinkled with wildflowers, half-circled by snowcapped rocky steeps.

"Now why do you suppose…." I said. "Where are we?"

"France," said Leslie. She said it without thinking and before I could ask her how she knew, she caught her breath. "Look."
She pointed to a cleft in the rock, where an old man in a coarse brown robe knelt on the ground near a small campfire. He was welding; brilliant yellow-white flickered and danced on the rocks behind him.
"What's a welder doing up here?" I asked. She watched him for a moment. "He's not welding" she said, as though she were remembering the scene instead of observing it. "He's praying."
She set off toward him and I followed, deciding to stay quiet. As I had seen myself in Attila, was my wife seeing herself in this hermit?

Closer and we saw sure enough, that was no welding torch. No sound, no smoke, it was a flaring sun-color pillar pulsing above the ground less than a yard from the elder.

"… And to the world shall you give, as you have received," came a gentle voice from the light. "Give to all who yearn to know the truth from whence we come, the reason for our being, and the course that lies ahead on the way to our forever home."

We stopped a few yards behind him, transfixed by the sight. I had seen that brilliance once before in my life, years ago, had been stunned by one accidental glimpse of what to this day I still call Love. The light we saw this moment was the same, so radiant it rendered the world a footnote, a dim asterisk.

Then, next instant, the light was gone. Beneath the place where it had been lay a sheaf of golden paper, a scripture in grand calligraphy. The man knelt silent, eyes closed, unaware of our presence. Leslie walked forward, reached for the glowing manuscript, picked it up. In this mystical place, her hand did not pass through the parchment.

Expecting runes or hieroglyphics, we found words in English. Of course, I thought. The old man would read them as French, a Persian as Farsi. So it must be with revelation — it's not the language that matters, but the communication of ideas.

You are creatures of light, we read. From light have you come, in light shall you go, and surrounding you through every step is the light of your infinite being.

She turned a page.

By your choice dwell you now in the world which you have created. What you hold in your heart shall be true, and what most you admire, that shall you become. Fear not, nor be dismayed at the appearance that is darkness, at the disguise that is evil, at the empty cloak that is death, for you have picked these for your challenges. They are the stones on which you choose to whet the keen edge of your spirit. Know that ever about you stands the reality of love, and each moment you have the power to transform your world by what you have learned.

The pages went on, hundreds of them. We leafed through, struck in awe.

You are life, inventing form. No more can you die on sword or years than you can die on doorways through which you walk, one room into another. Every room gives its word for you to speak, every passage its song for you to sing.

Leslie looked at me, her eyes luminous. If this writing could touch us so, I thought, we from the twentieth century, what effect would it have on people from the whatever-this-was … the twelfth!

We turned back to the manuscript. No words of ritual no directions for worship, no calling down fire and destruction on enemies, no disasters for unbelievers, no cruel Attila-gods. It didn't mention temples or priests or rabbis or congregations or choirs or costumes or holy days. It was scripture written for the loving inner being, and for that being only.

Turn these ideas loose in this century, I thought, a key to recognize our power over belief, unleash the power of love, and terror will vanish. With this, the world can sidestep the Dark Ages!

The old man opened his eyes, saw us at last, and stood as unafraid as if he'd read the scripture through. He glanced at me, looked a long moment at Leslie. "I am Jean-Paul Le Clerc," he said. "And you are angels."

Before we recovered from our puzzlement the man laughed, joyfully. "Did you notice," he said, "the Light?"

"Inspiration!" said my wife, handing him the golden pages.

"Inspiration, indeed." He bowed as though he remembered her, and she, at least, were an angel. "These words are key to the truth for any who will read, they are life to those who will listen. When I was a child, the Light promised that the pages would come to my hand on the night you should appear. Now that I am old, you have come, and they."

"They will change the world," I said.
He looked at me strangely. "No."
"But they were given to you…."
"In test," he said.
"Test?"

I have traveled far," he said, "I have studied scriptures of a hundred faiths, from Cathay to the Norselands." His eyes twinkled. "And in spite of my study, I have learned. Every grand religion begins in light. Yet only hearts hold light. Pages cannot."

"But you have in your hands…" I said. "You must read it. It's beautiful!"

"I have paper in my hands," said the elder. "Give these words to the world, and they will be loved and understood by those who already know their truth. But before we give them we must name them. And that will be their death."

"To name a beautiful thing is to kill it?"
He looked at me surprised. "To name a thing is harmless. To name these ideas is to create a religion."

"Why?"

He smiled, handing me the manuscript. "I give these pages to you…?"

"Richard," I told him.

"I give these pages directly from the Light of Love to you, Richard. Do you want to give them in turn to the world, to people yearning to know what they say, to ones who have not been privileged to stand at this place in the moment the gift was given? Or do you want to keep this writing for yourself alone?"

"I want to give them, of course!"

"And what will you call your gift?"

What is he getting at, I wondered. "Does it matter?"

"If you do not name it, others will. They will call it The Book of Richard."

"I see. All right. I'll call it anything … the pages."

"And will you safeguard The Pages? Or will you allow others to edit them, to change what they don't understand, to strike out what they please, whatever is not to their liking?"

"No! No changes. They were delivered from the light! No changes!"

"Are you sure? Not a line here and there, for good reason? 'Most people won't understand?' 'This might offend?' 'The message isn't clear?'"

"No changes!"

He raised his eyebrows, questioning. "Who are you to insist?"

I was here when they were given," I said. "I saw them appear, myself!"

"So," he said, "you have become the Keeper of the Pages?"

"Doesn't have to be me. It can be any one as long as they promise no changes."

"But someone is Keeper of the Pages?"

"Someone. I suppose."

"And here begins the Pageite priesthood. Those who give their lives to protect an order of thinking become the priests of that order. Yet any new order, any new way, is change. And change is the end of the world as it is."

"These pages are no threat," I said. "They're love and freedom!"

"And love and freedom are the end of fear and slavery."

"Of course!" I said, vexed. What was he getting at? Why was Leslie standing silent? Didn't she agree that this was....

"Those who profit from fear and slavery," said Le Clerc, "will they be happy with the message of the Pages?"

"Probably not, but we can't let this ... light ... be lost!"

"Will you promise to protect the light?' he said

"Of course!"

"The other Pageites, your friends, they'll protect it too?"

"Yes."

"And if the profiteers in fear and slavery convince the king of this land that you are dangerous, if they march on your house, if they come with swords, how are you going to protect the Pages?"

"I'll take them away! I'll escape!"

"And when you're followed, and caught, and cornered?"

"If I have to fight, I'll fight," I said. "There are principles more important than life. Some ideas are worth dying for."

"The old man sighed. "And so began the Pageite Wars," he said. "Armor and swords and shields and banners, horses and fire and blood in the streets. They will not be small wars. Thousands of true believers will join you, tens of thousands, swift and strong and smart. But the principles of the Pages challenge the rulers of every nation that keeps its power through fear and darkness. Tens of thousands will ride against you."

At last it began to dawn, what Le Clerc was trying to tell me.

"To be known," he went on, "to be distinguished from others, you will need a symbol. What symbol will you choose? What sign will you strike upon your banners?"

My heart sank under the weight of his words, but I struggled on. "The symbol of light," I said. "The sign of the flame."

"And so shall it be," he said, reading history unwritten, "that the Sign of the Flame shall meet the Sign of the Cross on the battlefields of France, and the Flame shall prevail, a glorious victory, and the first cities of the Cross shall be leveled by your pure fire. But the Cross shall join with the Crescent, and together their armies shall swarm in from the south and the east and down from the north, a hundred thousand armed men to your eighty thousand."

Oh, stop, I wanted to say. I know what comes next.

"And for every soldier of the Cross and warrior of the Crescent whom you kill protecting your gift, a hundred will hate your name. Their fathers and mothers, their wives and daughters and sons and friends will hate the Pageites and the cursed Pages for the murder of their loved ones, and every Pageite will despise every Christian and cursed Cross and every Moslem and cursed Crescent for the murder of their own."

"No!" I cried. Every word he said was true.

"And during the Wars, altars will spring up, cathedrals and spires will rise to enshrine the Pages. Those reaching for growth and understanding will find themselves burdened instead with new superstitions and new limits: bells and symbols, rules and chants, ceremonies and prayers and vestments, incense and offerings of gold. The heart of Pageism will turn from love to gold. Gold to build greater temples, gold to buy swords to convert the non-believers and save their souls."

"And when you die, First Keeper of the Pages, gold to build images of you. There will be towering statues, grand frescoes, paintings to commit this scene to immortal art. See, woven in this tapestry: here the Light, there the Pages, there the vault of the sky opened to Paradise. Here kneels Richard the Great in gleaming armor, here the lovely Angel of Wisdom, the Hallowed Pages in her hand; here old Le Clerc at his humble campfire in the mountains, witness to the vision."

No! I thought. Impossible!
But it wasn't impossible, it was inevitable.

"Give these pages to the world, and there shall be another mighty religion, another priesthood, another Us and another Them, one set against the other. In a hundred years, a million will have died for the words we hold in our hands; in a thousand years, tens of millions. All for this paper.

There was no trace of bitterness in his voice, nor did it grow cynical or weary. Jean-Paul Le Clerc was filled with a lifetime's learning, calm acceptance of what he had found.

Leslie shivered.

"Do you want my jacket?" I said.

"No thank you, wookie," she said. "It's not the cold."

"Not the cold," said Le Clerc. He stooped and picked a brand from his fire, raised it to touch the golden pages. "This will warm you."

"No!" I jerked the sheaf away. "Burn the truth?"

"The truth doesn't burn. The truth waits for anyone who wishes to find it," he said.

"Only these pages will burn. It is your choice. Would you like Pageism to become the next religion in this world?" He smiled. "You will be saints of the church. . . ."

I looked to Leslie, saw the horror in her eyes that I felt in my own. She took the brand from him, touched it to the corners of the parchment. The blaze grew to a wide sun-white blossom under our fingers, and in a moment we let the bright shards fall to the ground. They burned a moment longer and went dark.

The old man sighed his relief. "What a blessed evening!" he said. "How rarely are we given the chance to save the world from a new religion!"

Then he faced my wife, smiling hopefully. "We did save it?"

She smiled back at him. "We did. There is not a word in our history, Jean-Paul Le Clerc, of the Pageites or their wars."

They looked a tender goodbye to each other, skeptic to loving skeptic. Then with a small bow to both of us, the old man turned and walked up the mountain into the dark.

The fiery pages still burned in my mind, inspiration turned to ash. "But the ones who need what those pages had to say," I said to Leslie. "How can they ... how can we learn what was written there?"

"He's right," she said, looking after the man until she could see him no more, "whoever wants truth and light can find it for themselves."

"I'm not sure. Sometimes we need a teacher."

She turned to me. "Try this," she said. "Pretend that you honestly truly deeply want to know who you are, where you came from and why you're here. Pretend you're willing never to rest till you know." I nodded and imagined myself non-stop determined resolute, eager to learn, combing libraries for books and back-issues, haunting lectures and seminars, keeping diaries of my hopes and speculation, writing intuitions, meditating on mountaintops, following leads from dreams and coincidence, asking strangers — all the steps we take when learning matters more than anything. "OK."

"Now," she said, "can you imagine yourself not finding out?" Whuf, I thought. How this woman can make me see!

I bowed in answer. "My Lady Le Clerc, Princess of Knowing." She curtsied slowly in the dark. "My Lord Richard, Prince of the Flame."

Close and silent in the clear mountain air, I took her in my arms, the stars no longer above but around us. We were one with the stars, one with Le Clerc, with the pages and their love, one with Pye and Tink and Atkin and Attila, one with everything that is, that ever was or will be.

The Pageite wars
"One" by Richard Bach, 1988

Peace Prayer

Lord, make me an instrument of your peace:
where there is hatred, let me sow love;
where there is injury, pardon;
where there is doubt, faith;
where there is despair, hope;
where there is darkness, light;
where there is sadness, joy.

O divine Master, grant that I may not so much seek
to be consoled as to console,
to be understood as to understand,
to be loved as to love.
For it is in giving that we receive,
it is in pardoning that we are pardoned,
and it is in dying that we are born to eternal life.
Amen.

St. Francis

"The reason birds have faith is because they have wings, for to have faith is to have wings."

St. Francis of Assisi

LIFE

Life is an opportunity, benefit from it.
Life is a beauty, admire it.
Life is a dream, realize it.
Life is a challenge, meet it.
Life is a duty, complete it.
Life is a game, play it.
Life is a promise, fulfill it.
Life is sorrow, overcome it.
Life is a song, sing it.
Life is a struggle, accept it.
Life is a tragedy, confront it.
Life is an adventure, dare it.
Life is luck, make it.
Life is life, fight for it!

Mother Teresa

"The proof of a Creator is obvious: we enjoy everything that this world gives us, for free to enjoy, from food to all the miracles we take for granted without comprehending that SOMEONE put them there."

Norb Svanascini

"Important principles may and must be inflexible."

Abraham Lincoln

O f all the dispositions and habits which least to political prosperity, Religion and morality are indispensable supports. In vain would that man claim the tribute of Patriotism who should labor to subvert these great Pillars of human happiness -- these firmest props of the duties of men and citizens. The mere Politician, equally with the pious man ought to respect and to cherish them. ... Let it simply be asked where is the security for property, for reputation, for life, if the sense of religious obligation desert the oaths...? Let us with caution indulge the opposition, that morality can be maintained without religion. Reason and experience both forbid us to expect that national morality can prevail in exclusion of religious principle.

George Washington

"Every new child born, brings the message that God is not yet discouraged by man."

Rabindranath Tagore

In the absence of a God figure, humans might have to do what their heart tells them.

Author Unknown

A loaf of bread bounced from a basket as a baker's truck turned the corner too quickly. When the loaf hit the pavement, a crumb broke off and lay beside it.

Almost instantly, three sparrows made a swoop for the crumb. When the contest was over, two of the birds flew away without a bite, and the other one carried off a meager breakfast. The loaf was untouched, unnoticed. The crumb was worthwhile as a sampling; it was nothing as a prize. Just a little wider range of vision, just a little more faith, and each bird would have been fully satisfied and rewarded. How often our own eyes-those of individuals and of nations-are blurred to our own opportunities while we fight for crumbs.

Catholic Quote

RECOMMENDED MOVIES

Lilies of the Field
Ben Hur
Field of Dreams
Hannah and Her Sisters

CHAPTER 7

LIFE

The Magic Bank Account

Imagine that you had won the following *PRIZE* in a contest: Each morning your bank would deposit $86,400 in your private account for your use. However, this prize has Rules.

The set of Rules:
1. Everything that you didn't spend during each day would be taken away from you.
2. You may not simply transfer money into some other account.
3. You may only spend It.
4. Each morning upon awakening, the bank opens your account with another $86,400 for that day.
5. The bank can end the game without warning; at any time, it can say, "Game Over!" It can close the account, and you will not receive a new one.

What would you personally do?

You would buy anything and everything you wanted, right? Not only for yourself, but for all the people you love and care for. Even for people you don't know, because you couldn't possibly spend it all on yourself - right?

You would try to spend every penny, and use it all, because you knew it would be replenished in the morning, right?

Actually, this game is real!

Each of us is already a winner of this *PRIZE.*

We just can't seem to see it.

The PRIZE is "TIME."

1. Each morning we awaken to Receive 86,400 seconds as a gift of Life.
2. And when we go to sleep at Night, any remaining time is Not credited to us.
3. What we haven't used up that Day is forever lost.
4. Yesterday is forever Gone.
5. Each morning the account is Refilled, but the bank can dissolve your account at any time without warning...

SO, what will YOU do with your 86,400 seconds?

Those seconds are worth so much More than the same amount in dollars. Think about it and remember to Enjoy every second of your life, because time races by so much quicker than You think.

So take care of yourself, be Happy, love deeply and enjoy life!

Here's wishing you a wonderful And beautiful day.

Start spending....
"Don't complain about growing old – some people don't get the privilege!"

Author Unknown

It was found in the billfold of Coach Paul Bear Bryant, Alabama, after he died in 1982

I have always pitied those that have too much. A few years back, I had a very fine young man that worked for me. He wasn't formally educated, come from a very poor background, hardly had any conveniences, let alone luxuries, while growing up; but he made up all of his shortcomings by always being happy and always going out of his way to please the customer and me, his employer.

One day, I had to visit a client and he went with me. Upon entering my client's office, I noticed 3 pieces of modern art that were very expensive and I casually mentioned to my employee that those paintings were probably worth $50,000 dollars. He looked at them and said something that changed my way of thinking forever. I quote: "It's funny what people do with their money, when they have too much of it."

He was right. When you think about it, it is silly what people do with their money when they have too much; they buy jewelry, so called "art," huge homes, clothing with other peoples' names on

them, etc. etc. This simple man saw through the circus we call
success because he had the real luxury of knowing what was really
important.

Norb Svanascini

FRANKIE

He wasn't here four years ago,
He just wasn't here.

His smile wasn't here
His tears weren't here
His laugh, his kisses,
His small body sleeping, his running,

None of it was here.

Now Frankie is here,
And all those things that weren't,
Are here now.

Some call it normal,
Some don't even care.

Could it be that miracles are so commonplace,
That few notice?

Norb Svanascini

Yesterday, when I was 11 years old I arrived to this country. I've never understood why humanity doesn't treat greed, or the quest for power, as the disease it really is, similar to alcoholism or even cocaine.

Norb Svanascini

Things I Learned in Southern Indiana

You might wonder why I specify "Southern Indiana" instead of just "Indiana." For all of you that don't know it, Southern Indiana is the place where the heart is down south but geography says it's in the North.

There was a Country Store owned by a man called "Honey Jones," and the reason he was called this is because when you came into his store he called you "Honey", no matter who you were. I remember Honey Jones not only because of his name, but also for a plaque behind the cash register that read "In Jesus we trust, all others pay cash." Good advice if you run a business; and this brings us to another anecdote:

My father's employer took a lot of people to a circus, and during a very hard and dangerous stunt, he looked at us and said: "It's funny what people will do for money."

Never forget this: It's funny what people will do for money.
It's even sad.

Norb Svanascini

When an old man died in the geriatric ward of a nursing home in Grass Valley, California, it was believed that he had nothing left of any value.

Later, when the nurses were going through his meager possessions, they found this poem. Its quality and content so impressed the staff that copies were made and distributed to every nurse in the hospital.
One nurse took her copy to Missouri.

The old man's sole bequest to posterity has since appeared in the Christmas edition of the News Magazine of the St. Louis Association for Mental Health. A slide presentation has also been made based on his simple, but eloquent, poem.

And this little old man, with nothing left to give to the world, is now the author of this 'anonymous' poem winging across the Internet.

CRABBY OLD MAN...

What do you see nurses? ... What do you see?
What are you thinking ... when you're looking at me?
A crabby old man ... not very wise,
Uncertain of habit ... with faraway eyes?

Who dribbles his food ... and makes no reply.
When you say in a loud voice ... 'I do wish you'd try!'
Who seems not to notice ... the things that you do.
And forever is losing ... a sock or shoe?

Who, resisting or not … lets you do as you will,
With bathing and feeding … The long day to fill?
Is that what you're thinking?… Is that what you see?
Then open your eyes, nurse… you're not looking at me.
I'll tell you who I am … As I sit here so still,
As I do at your bidding, … as I eat at your will.
I'm a small child of Ten … with a father and mother,
Brothers and sisters … who love one another.

A young boy of Sixteen … with wings on his feet.
Dreaming that soon now … a lover he'll meet.
A groom soon at Twenty … my heart gives a leap.
Remembering, the vows … that I promised to keep.

At Twenty-Five, now … I have young of my own.
Who need me to guide … And a secure happy home.
A man of Thirty … My young now grown fast,
Bound to each other … With ties that should last.

At Forty, my young sons … have grown and are gone,
But my woman's beside me … to see I don't mourn.
At Fifty, once more, babies play 'round my knee,
Again, we know children … My loved one and me.

Dark days are upon me … my wife is now dead.
I look at the future … shudder with dread.
For my young are all rearing … young of their own.
And I think of the years … and the love that I've known.

I'm now an old man … and nature is cruel.
Tis jest to make old age … look like a fool.

The body, it crumbles ... grace and vigor, depart.
There is now a stone ... where I once had a heart.

But inside this old carcass ... a young guy still dwells,
And now and again ... my battered heart swells.
I remember the joys ... I remember the pain.
And I'm loving and living ... life over again.

I think of the years, all too few ... gone too fast.
And accept the stark fact ... that nothing can last.
So open your eyes, people ... open and see.
Not a crabby old man ... Look closer ... see ME!!

Vincent Guarisco

As an atomic veteran who founded and directed the International Alliance of Atomic veterans, my father Anthony Guarisco, is a WWII and Korean War veteran who walked on the ashes of Hiroshima. He also got to meet Tsue Hayashi in Japan. I remember well my father telling me her story. May it leave a mental imprint on your soul (as it did mine) to never allow another nuclear bomb to explode ever.

Tsue Hayashi's only child was named Kayoko. In August 1945, Kayoko was fifteen years old. Like many her age, she had been mobilized for the war effort. She worked at the Shiroyama Primary School, which had been converted into a torpedo-assembly plant. The school was located in Nagasaki's Urakami district, 3.5 Kilometers from her home.

In a 1985 interview which was translated by Setsumi Del Tredici, Tsue Hayashi shared her riveting story. It was originally published in Tredici's 1987 book, "At Work in the Fields of the Bomb." At the time of the interview, Tsue was 84 years of age:

Tredici: The story of Kayoko's cherry trees is well known in Nagasaki, but outside Nagasaki not many people have heard of it. . .

Tsue: That is right. It is not known. I never meant it to be famous. I'd prefer people to leave Kayoko's cherry trees alone. The story came from my desire to pray for Kayoko's spirit and for everyone who died in the bomb.

Tredici: How does it begin?

Tsue: On the morning of August 9, I gave Kayoko her lunch box, and she went out of the house to go to work at the Shiroyama Primary School. A few minutes later she came back and put her lunch box down. I asked her, "What is wrong?" She said, "I don't feel like going to work today." This was unusual. Kayoko was a very serious girl. She always worked hard. This was the first time she had said something like this. I wanted to tell her, "Please take the day off," but I didn't. Her birthday was coming in two days, and I wanted her to take a day off then. If she took a day off now, that would make two days in one week. So I told her to go to work, and in two days she would have a holiday. She picked up her lunch box and went to work. I am the one who sent her away. I regret and regret and regret this.

Later that morning the bomb fell. At first I did not realize it was an atomic bomb. I just noticed bright and flashing, like sparks from a trolley car, and I heard thunder. I ran out of the house without my shoes on and saw the sky over Ukakami full of black smoke. It was unusual. My first thought was to get Kayoko. I started making my way toward Urakami, but the chief of my block saw me and called out, "Where are you going?" I told him, "Kayoki is in Urakami!" He grabbed me and said, "You'll die if you go there!" I stood there for a long time. The smoke began to turn into flames. I went home. People with burns on their faces and backs started going past my house. Some had skin hanging down like rags. I asked them, "How is Urakami?" And, "Have you seen Kayoko? She was working at the Shiroyama Primary School." They told me that a big bomb had been dropped and that Urakami had been destroyed.

The whole night I waited for Kayoko on the front porch. I kept praying for her to be alive. The morning after the bomb, and every day after that, from early morning until evening, I walked all over the city looking for Kayoko. I saw many people suffering and dying. It was very sad. I felt deeply the severe power of the A-bomb. I cannot remember seeing a single other person walking. Maybe this is because of the rumor that you will die sooner if you go into Urakami. There were no trees there, no grass, only a lot of broken roof tiles. And many corpses. I thought, "I've heard of hell. It must be like this." Some of the people were still dying. When I walked past them they would say, "Give me water. Please help me." I could only say "I'm sorry. I have no water. I can't help you. Forgive me. I have to look for my child."

When I was looking for my child I kept thinking about the wisdom of mankind. I wondered, "What on earth is this wisdom of mankind?" Whatever it was, I hated it. It wasn't the bad people who were killed. The A-bomb killed everybody. Even condemned criminal have a better death than the people I saw suffering. I couldn't help them at all; I had to walk right through them. My feet were hurt and bleeding, but I kept thinking stubbornly about the wisdom of mankind. Who invented this bomb? If they had such great brains, why couldn't they also invent a way to help the victims recover? I knew there would be no answer to my question. I think mankind opened the lid of the box that God said not to open in the Bible. I hope mankind never uses the A-bomb again.

Day after day, for twenty-one days, I wandered, seeking my Kayoko. It was the middle of summer and the days were very hot. One time I was looking for Kayoko in the mountains and I saw a young woman with a cotton shawl over her head, nursing her baby. I was frightened and wondered if she was a real human being. I went closer. I found out she was not a person in this world anymore. It was a corpse. When I saw that, I thought, "How Miserable!" Maybe only women will understand the feeling of nursing a baby. It was a very pure and innocent time. It is like heaven in world. The A-bomb killed this woman in that pure and innocent moment.

At first I was looking for a live child, but about halfway through my search I started looking for her among the corpses. But the corpses were so burned you could recognize only the shape of the skull. I decided to look at the corpses' teeth. My child had a row of teeth that was different from others'. Her front bottom teeth came out a little farther than usual. She was also starting treatment on a back tooth. So I opened the mouths of corpses to look at their teeth. Some of the corpses' mouths were closed very tightly. I had to pry them open.

One day I found a corpse whose teeth looked like my child's. I wasn't sure, though, because Kayoko's back tooth had not received a real filling yet, but the corpse whose teeth were like Kayoko's looked like it had a filling. Still I thought, "It's Kayoko," and I brought the remains back home. I had a funeral ceremony with my neighbors.

When I finished the funeral, my heart would not become calm. I had a dream at that time. In the dream I saw Kayoko wandering in the ruins. That made me think, "Kayoko is still waiting for me out there. Maybe she is even still alive, just barely breathing, and she can't call out." So I kept looking for my child every day, even after the funeral.

At last I found my real child. It finally happened twenty-one days after the bomb exploded. I found her on the top floor of the Shiroyama Primary School. This was the third time I had gone up there to look for her. To get to the third floor, I had to crawl, because the stairway had been destroyed.

Tredici: How did you know it was the real Kayoko this time?

Tsue: During the war I made an air-raid hood for Kayoko out of my cotton Kimono. I heard cotton did not burn easily. I sewed a small notebook into the top part of the hood. In the notebook I had written my last will and testament. I told Kayoko: If I die, you should live in such-and-such a way. I have left your belongings under my parents' place in the country. When the war is over, get them. Your home's economical condition is such-and-such. Learn this condition and live according to it. You should never commit suicide, even if I die and you become very sad. Keep living firmly.

You were born with the ability to survive.

When I went upstairs this time at the Shiroyama Primary School, I noticed a piece of that air-raid hood. I said, "What's that?" and ran over to it. There I found the upper part of my child's body. It was half burned. There was no lower part remaining. Everything else on the third floor had been burned completely. Other people's bones were burned and had become like pieces of small gravel. But my child's bones remained intact, even though there was no meat on them. And the shape of my child's open mouth formed an "ah" sound, as if she was saying "Ka-a-a-a." When I saw that, I thought my child must have been calling "O-Ka-cha-ma" (Mommy) before she died.

Tredici: Was the notebook still in the cotton hood?

Tsue: Yes, it hadn't been burned. I was very sad to pick up my last will and testament again in this place. I wrapped up my child's bones in cloth. To get down to the ground floor I had to slide down on my bottom, pulling the cloth bundle behind me. On the ground, I cremated my child. When I got home I came down with a very high fever, and I had to stay in bed.

Tredici: What happened with the remains of the other child?

Tsue: I buried her in the same grave as Kayoko's. So the unknown girl was enshrined as one of my family's deceased. When the festival of the dead comes I have a priest pray for the unknown girl, too. Do you know what Ta-mu-ke is? It means to offer something to dead people, like flowers or cookies. I still offer cooked rice and tea every day.

Tredici: For Kayoko?

Tsue: Yes, but for many dead people everywhere, I walked through them, crying. When the war was over, I eagerly wanted to make some kind of offering. I thought about it over and over. I decided I'd like to plant cherry trees to go around the school. I wanted to do this for their souls.

Tredici: For the souls of. . .

Tsue: For the souls of everyone. If it were only for Kayoko I wouldn't have dared to ask for permission to plant the trees. Thousands of people died there were so many corpses it was hard not to step on them. I wanted to offer something to all those people. The trees were for everybody. Do you understand?
The Shiroyama teacher said, "All right, you may plant cherry trees." But there were no young cherry trees in Nagasaki at that time. A gardener told me, "There's not even food here, not to mention young cherry trees!" I asked the gardener and his son to go to Kurume to buy them. They planted the cheery trees around the school. Those trees were beautiful when they bloomed.

Tredici: Thank you for telling your story. I learned today that Kayoko's cherry trees were not only for Kayoko, but for everyone.

Tsue: Do you know something? I never named them "Kayoko's Cherry Trees." The school named them that. I would have called them something like "Ta-mu-ke no sakura" ("Cherry Tree Offering for the Dead"). I didn't build the monument either. The school put it in. This whole thing has become more and more famous, and I am somewhat embarrassed by it.

Tsue Hayashi
interview by Setsumi Del Tredici

I was a young boy, maybe 12 or 13, and my father who came to America because he was in love with the country he chose because of its ideals, took me to a local hardware store to buy a hammer. He proceeded to the area where the hammers were displayed and picked up a Stanley hammer which was the best one and, even at that time, it cost 5 dollars. He turned to me and said, "You see son, this is what makes a great country, when it can produce a hammer like this." I never forgot that lesson, that moment when someone teaches something that no school or experience can equal, the simple logic that something as fundamental as a hammer, can also be the foundation of a great country. Anyone could own a Stanley hammer, whether rich or poor, you couldn't buy a better hammer. He's been gone for quite a while now, but the lesson and the Stanley are mine, both still in perfect condition and waiting for me to pass them on.

Norb Svanascini

D o not believe in anything simply because you have heard it. Do not believe in traditions because they have been handed down for many generations. Do not believe anything because it is spoken and rumored by many. Do not believe in anything because it is written in your religious books. Do not believe in anything merely on the authority of your teachers and elders. But after observation and analysis, when you find that anything agrees with reason and is conducive to the good and the benefit of one and all, then accept it and live up to it.

Buddha

1. Take into account that great love and great achievements involve great risk.
2. When you lose, don't lose the lesson.
3. Follow the three Rs:
    - Respect for self,
    - Respect for others,
    - Responsibility for all your actions.
4. Remember that not getting what you want is sometimes a wonderful stroke of luck.
5. Learn the rules so you know how to break them properly.
6. Don't let a little dispute injure a great friendship.
7. When you realize you've made a mistake, take immediate steps to correct it.
8. Spend some time alone every day.
9. Open your arms to change, but don't let go of your values
10. Remember that silence is sometimes the best answer.
11. Live a good, honorable life. Then when you get older and think back, you'll be able to enjoy it a second time.
12. A loving atmosphere in your home is the foundation for your life.
13. In disagreements with loved ones, deal only with the current situation. Don't bring up the past.
14. Share your knowledge. It's a way to achieve immortality.
15. Be gentle with the earth.
16. Once a year, go someplace you've never been before.
17. Remember that the best relationship is one in which your love for each other exceeds your need for each other.
18. Judge your success by what you had to give up in order to get it.
19. Approach love and cooking with reckless abandon.

Dalai Lama

"Often, the test of courage is not to die, but to live."

Vittorio Alfieri

S he was shy of 95 years by two weeks; she saw the radio, tele-phone, refrigerator, airplane travel, television, computers, and so on and so on. Probably the greatest span of humanity in the history of the world. Married devotedly to the same man for 57 years, following wherever he went. Had her idiosyncrasies, like all of us, but lived a full life. Left a family that by in large is a contributing factor to society; not one of them ever on public dole or useless professions, no drunks or drug addicts, no criminal of-fences. In short, the world is better off because of her.

May heaven accept her; she contributed and if there is a guideline to qualify entrance to that promised life it should be that.
May God Bless her.

Norb Svanascini

W hen I was quite young, my father had one of the first tele-phones in our neighborhood. I remember the polished, old case fastened to the wall. The shiny receiver hung on the side of the box. I was too little to reach the telephone, but used to listen with fascination when my mother talked to it.

Then I discovered that somewhere inside the wonderful device lived an amazing person. Her name was "Information Please" and there was nothing she did not know. Information Please could supply anyone's number and the correct time.

My personal experience with the genie-in-a-bottle came one day while my mother was visiting a neighbor. Amusing myself at the tool bench in the basement, I whacked my finger with a hammer, the pain was terrible, but there seemed no point in crying because there was no one home to give sympathy.

I walked around the house sucking my throbbing finger, finally arriving at the stairway. The telephone! Quickly, I ran for the footstool in the parlor and dragged it to the landing. Climbing up, I unhooked the receiver in the parlor and held it to my ear. "Information, please" I said into the mouthpiece just above my head. A click or two and a small clear voice spoke into my ear, "Information."

"I hurt my finger..." I wailed into the phone, the tears came readily enough now that I had an audience.

"Isn't your mother home?" came the question.

"Nobody's home but me," I blubbered.

"Are you bleeding?" the voice asked.

"No," I replied.

"I hit my finger with the hammer and it hurts."

"Can you open the icebox?" she asked. I said I could.

"Then chip off a little bit of ice and hold it to your finger," said the voice.

After that, I called "Information Please" for everything. I asked her for help with my geography, and she told me where Philadelphia was. She helped me with my math. She told me my pet chipmunk that I had caught in the park just the day before, would eat fruit and nuts. Then, there was the time Petey, our pet canary, died. I called "Information Please," and told her the sad story. She listened, and then said things grown-ups say to soothe a child. But I was not consoled. I asked her, "Why is it that birds should sing so beautifully and bring joy to all families, only to end up as a heap of feathers on the bottom of a cage?"

She must have sensed my deep concern, for she said quietly, "Wayne, always remember that there are other worlds to sing in." Somehow I felt better.

Another day I was on the telephone, "Information Please." "Information," said in the now familiar voice.

"How do I spell fix?" I asked. All this took place in a small town in the Pacific Northwest. When I was nine years old, we moved across the country to Boston. I missed my friend very much. "Information Please" belonged in that old wooden box back home and I somehow never thought of trying the shiny new phone that sat on the table in the hall.

As I grew into my teens, the memories of those childhood conversations never really left me. Often, in moments of doubt and perplexity, I would recall the serene sense of security I had then. I appreciated now how patient, understanding, and kind she was to have spent her time on a little boy.

A few years later, on my way west to college, my plane put down in Seattle. I had about a half-hour or so between planes. I spent 15 minutes or so on the phone with my sister, who lived there now. Then without thinking what I was doing, I dialed my hometown operator and said,

"Information Please." Miraculously, I heard the small, clear voice I knew so well... "Information." I hadn't planned this, but I heard myself saying, "Could you please tell me how to spell fix?" There was a long pause.

Then came the soft spoken answer, "I guess your finger must have healed by now."

I laughed, "So it's really you," I said. "I wonder if you have any idea how much you meant to me during that time?"

"I wonder," she said, "if you know how much your call meant to me. I never had any children and I used to look forward to your calls."

I told her how often I had thought of her over the years and I asked if I could call her again when I came back to visit my sister.

"Please do," she said. "Just ask for Sally."

Three months later I was back in Seattle... A different voice answered "Information." ...I asked for Sally.

"Are you a friend?" she said.

"Yes, a very old friend," I answered.

"I'm sorry to have to tell you this," she said. "Sally had been working part-time the last few years because she was sick. She died five weeks ago." Before I could hang up she said, "Wait a minute, did you say your name was Wayne?"

"Yes." I answered.

"Well, Sally left a message for you. She wrote it down in case you called. Let me read it to you. The note said, 'Tell him there are other worlds to sing in. He'll know what I mean.'"

I thanked her and hung up. I knew what Sally meant.

Never underestimate the impression you may make on others.
Whose life have you touched today?

Lifting you on eagle's wings.
May you find the joy and peace you long for.
Life is a journey ... NOT a guided tour.

Paul Villard

During my second month of nursing school, our professor gave us a pop quiz. I was a conscientious student and had breezed through the questions, until I read the last one: "What is the first name of the woman who cleans the school?" Surely, this was some kind of joke.

I had seen the cleaning woman several times. She was tall, dark-haired and in her 50s, but how would I know her name? I handed in my paper, leaving the last question blank.

Just before class ended, one student asked if the last question would count toward our quiz grade. "Absolutely," said the professor. "In your careers, you will meet many people. All are significant. They deserve your attention and care, even if all you do is smile and say 'Hello.'" I've never forgotten that lesson. I also learned her name was Dorothy.

This came from my grandmother, and it was the best advice I ever got.

Queen Elizabeth II was being coronated and my grandmother and I were watching the coronation on TV. I made the comment "she must be a very important person", and at that moment she uttered the words that have made me comfortable with any person I've ever met, whether billionaires or poor, whether educated or not, politician or honest man, etc.

"She makes caca just like you or me."
When someone that thinks he or she is something special I automatically think of them sitting on a toilet, and the aura disappears instantly.

Amy Taylor

Speaking of Rock 'n' Roll:

"The most brutal, ugly, desperate, vicious form of expression it has been my misfortune to hear."

Frank Sinatra

"It's more important to be human than to be important."

Arnold Svanascini

A while back, there was a story about Reuben Gonzolas, who was in the final match of his first professional racquetball tournament. He was playing the perennial champion for his first shot at a victory on the pro circuit. At match point in the fifth and final game, Gonzolas made a super "kill shot" into the front corner to win the tournament. The referee called it good, and one of the linemen confirmed the shot was a winner.

But after a moment's hesitation, Gonzolas turned and declared that his shot had skipped into the wall, hitting the floor first. As a result, the serve went to his opponent, who went on to win the match.

Reuben Gonzolas walked off the court; everyone was stunned. The next issue of a leading racquetball magazine featured Gonzolas on its cover. The lead editorial searched and questioned for an explanation for the first ever occurrence on the professional racquetball circuit. Who could ever imagine it in any sport or endeavor? Here was a player with everything officially in his favor, with victory in his grasp, who disqualifies himself at match point and loses.

When asked why he did it, Gonzolas replied, "It was the only thing I could do to maintain my integrity."

While at the park one day, a woman sat down next to a man on a bench near a playground. "That's my son over there," she said, pointing to a little boy in a red sweater who was gliding down the slide.

"He's a fine looking boy" the man said. "That's my daughter on the bike in the white dress." Then, looking at his watch, he called to his daughter. "What do you say we go, Melissa?"
Melissa pleaded, "Just five more minutes, Dad. Please? Just five more minutes." The man nodded and Melissa continued to ride her bike to her heart's content. Minutes passed and the father stood and called again to his daughter. "Time to go now?"
Again Melissa pleaded, "Five more minutes, Dad. Just five more minutes." The man smiled and said, "OK."

"My, you certainly are a patient father," the woman responded. The man smiled and then said, "Her older brother Tommy was killed by a drunk driver last year while he was riding his bike near here. I never spent much time with Tommy and now I'd give anything for just five more minutes with him. I've vowed not to make the same mistake with Melissa. She thinks she has five more minutes to ride her bike. The truth is, I get five more minutes to watch her play."

"Life is all about making priorities, what are your priorities? Give someone you love 5 more minutes of your time today!"

Author Unknown

To laugh often and much; to win the respect of intelligent people and the affection of children; to earn the appreciation of honest critics and endure the betrayal of false friends; to appreciate beauty, to find the best in others; to leave the world a bit better, whether by a healthy child, a garden patch or a redeemed social condition; to know even one life has breathed easier because you have lived. This is to have succeeded.

Ralph Waldo Emerson

One day a man saw an old lady, stranded on the side of the road but, even in the dim light of day, he could see she needed help. So he pulled up in front of her Mercedes and got out. His Pontiac was still sputtering when he approached her.

Even with the smile on his face, she was worried. No one had stopped to help for the last hour or so. Was he going to hurt her? He didn't look safe; he looked poor and hungry.

He could see that she was frightened, standing out there in the cold. He knew how she felt. It was those chills which only fear can put in you.

He said, "I'm here to help you, ma'am. Why don't you wait in the car where it's warm? By the way, my name is Bryan Anderson." Well, all she had was a flat tire but, for an old lady, that was bad enough. Bryan crawled under the car looking for a place to put the jack, skinning his knuckles a time or two. Soon he was able to change the tire but he had to get dirty and his hands hurt.

As he was tightening up the lug nuts, she rolled down the window and began to talk to him. She told him that she was from St. Louis and was only just passing through. She couldn't thank him enough for coming to her aid.

Bryan just smiled as he closed her trunk. The lady asked how much she owed him. Any amount would have been all right with her. She already imagined all the awful things that could have happened had he not stopped. Bryan never thought twice about being paid. This was not a job to him. This was helping someone in need and, God knows, there were plenty who had given him a hand in the past. He had lived his whole life that way and it never occurred to him to act any other way.

He told her that if she really wanted to pay him back the next time she saw someone who needed help she could give that person the

147

assistance they needed. Bryan added, "And think of me."

He waited until she started her car and drove off. It had been a cold and depressing day but he felt good as he headed for home disappearing into the twilight.

A few miles down the road, the lady saw a small cafe. She went in to grab a bite to eat and take the chill off before she made the last leg of her trip home. It was a dingy looking restaurant. Outside were two old gas pumps. The whole scene was unfamiliar to her. The waitress came over and brought a clean towel to wipe her wet hair. She had a sweet smile, one that even being on her feet for the whole day couldn't erase. The lady noticed the waitress was nearly eight months pregnant but she never let the strain and aches change her attitude. The old lady wondered how someone who had so little could be so giving to a stranger. Then she remembered Bryan.

After the lady finished her meal, she paid with a hundred dollar bill. The waitress quickly went to get change for her hundred dollar bill but the old lady had slipped right out the door. She was gone by the time the waitress came back. The waitress wondered where the lady could be. Then she noticed something written on the napkin.

There were tears in her eyes when she read what the lady wrote: "You don't owe me anything. I have been there too. Somebody once helped me out, the way I'm helping you. If you really want to pay me back, here is what you do: Do not let this chain of love end with you."

Under the napkin were four more $100 bills.

Well, there were tables to clear, sugar bowls to fill, and people to serve, but the waitress made it through another day. That night, when she got home from work and climbed into bed, she was thinking about the money and what the lady had written. How could the lady have known how much she and her husband needed it? With the baby due next month, it was going to be hard...

She knew how worried her husband was and, as he lay sleeping next to her, she gave him a soft kiss and whispered soft and low, "Everything's going to be all right. I love you, Bryan Anderson."

There is an old saying, "What goes around comes around." Today I sent you this story and I'm asking you to pass it on. Let this light shine. God works in mysteries ways and sometimes puts people in our lives for a reason.

Jonnie Barnett and Rory Lee
Chicken Soup for the Country Soul

This is a wonderful piece by Michael Gartner, editor of newspapers large and small and president of NBC News. In 1997, he won the Pulitzer Prize for editorial writing. It is well worth reading, and a few good chuckles are guaranteed. Here goes...

My father never drove a car. Well, that's not quite right. I should say I never saw him drive a car.

He quit driving in 1927, when he was 25 years old, and the last car he drove was a 1926 Whippet.

"In those days," he told me when he was in his 90s, "to drive a car you had to do things with your hands, and do things with your feet, and look every which way, and I decided you could walk through life and enjoy it or drive through life and miss it."

At which point my mother, a sometimes salty Irishwoman, chimed in: "Oh, bull shit!" she said. "He hit a horse."

"Well," my father said, "there was that, too."

So my brother and I grew up in a household without a car. The neighbors all had cars the Kollingses next door had a green 1941 Dodge, the VanLaninghams across the street a gray 1936 Plymouth, the Hopsons two doors down a black 1941 Ford but we had none.

My father, a newspaperman in Des Moines, would take the streetcar to work and, often as not, walk the 3 miles home. If he took the streetcar home, my mother and brother and I would walk the three blocks to the streetcar stop, meet him and walk home together.

My brother, David, was born in 1935, and I was born in 1938, and sometimes, at dinner, we'd ask how come all the neighbors had cars but we had none. "No one in the family drives," my mother would explain, and that was that.

But, sometimes, my father would say, "But as soon as one of you boys turns 16, we'll get one." It was as if he wasn't sure which one of us would turn 16 first.

But, sure enough, my brother turned 16 before I did, so in 1951 my parents bought a used 1950 Chevrolet from a friend who ran the parts department at a Chevy dealership downtown.

It was a four-door, white model, stick shift, fender skirts, loaded with everything, and, since my parents didn't drive, it more or less became my brother's car. Having a car but not being able to drive didn't bother my father, but it didn't make sense to my mother.

So in 1952, when she was 43 years old, she asked a friend to teach her to drive. She learned in a nearby cemetery, the place where I learned to drive the following year and where, a generation later, I took my two sons to practice driving. The cemetery probably was my father's idea. "Who can your mother hurt in the cemetery?" I remember him saying more than once.

For the next 45 years or so, until she was 90, my mother was the driver in the family. Neither she nor my father had any sense of direction, but he loaded up on maps though they seldom left the city limits and appointed himself navigator. It seemed to work. Still, they both continued to walk a lot. My mother was a devout Catholic, and my father an equally devout agnostic, an arrangement that didn't seem to bother either of them through their 75 years of marriage.
(Yes, 75 years, and they were deeply in love the entire time.)
He retired when he was 70, and nearly every morning for the next 20 years or so, he would walk with her the mile to St. Augustin's Church.

She would walk down and sit in the front pew, and he would wait in the back until he saw which of the parish's two priests was on duty that morning. If it was the pastor, my father then would go out and take a 2-mile walk, meeting my mother at the end of the service and walking her home.

If it was the assistant pastor, he'd take just a 1-mile walk and then head back to the church. He called the priests "Father Fast" and "Father Slow."

After he retired, my father almost always accompanied my mother whenever she drove anywhere, even if he had no reason to go along. If she were going to the beauty parlor, he'd sit in the car and read, or go take a stroll or, if it was summer, have her keep the engine running so he could listen to the Cubs game on the radio. In the evening, then, when I'd stop by, he'd explain: "The Cubs lost again. The millionaire on second base made a bad throw to the millionaire on first base, so the multimillionaire on third base scored."

If she were going to the grocery store, he would go along to carry the bags out and to make sure she loaded up on ice cream. As I said, he was always the navigator, and once, when he was 95 and she was 88 and still driving, he said to me, "Do you want to know the secret of a long life?"

"I guess so," I said, knowing it probably would be something bizarre.

"No left turns," he said. "What?" I asked.

"No left turns," he repeated. "Several years ago, your mother and I read an article that said most accidents that old people are in happen when they turn left in front of oncoming traffic. As you get older, your eyesight worsens, and you can lose your depth perception, it said. So your mother and I decided never again to make a left turn."

"What?" I said again.

"No left turns," he said. "Think about it. Three rights are the same as a left, and that's a lot safer. So we always make three rights."

"You're kidding!" I said, and I turned to my mother for support.

"No," she said, "your father is right. We make three rights. It works." But then she added: "Except when your father loses count." I was driving at the time, and I almost drove off the road as I started laughing. "Loses count?" I asked.

"Yes," my father admitted, "that sometimes happens. But it's not a problem. You just make seven rights, and you're okay again."

I couldn't resist. "Do you ever go for 11?" I asked.

"No," he said "If we miss it at seven, we just come home and call it a bad day. Besides, nothing in life is so important it can't be put off another day or another week."

My mother was never in an accident, but one evening she handed me her car keys and said she had decided to quit driving. That was in 1999, when she was 90. She lived four more years, until 2003. My father died the next year, at 102.

They both died in the bungalow they had moved into in 1937 and bought a few years later for $3,000. (Sixty years later, my brother and I paid $8,000 to have a shower put in the tiny bathroom the house had never had one. My father would have died then and there if he knew the shower cost nearly three times what he paid for the house.) He continued to walk daily he had me get him a treadmill when he was 101 because he was afraid he'd fall on the icy sidewalks but wanted to keep exercising and he was of sound mind and sound body until the moment he died.

One September afternoon in 2004, he and my son went with me when I had to give a talk in a neighboring town, and it was clear to all three of us that he was wearing out, though we had the usual wide-ranging conversation about politics and newspapers and things in the news. A few weeks earlier, he had told my son, "You know, Mike, the first hundred years are a lot easier than the second hundred." At one point in our drive that Saturday, he said, "You know, I'm probably not going to live much longer."

"You're probably right," I said.

"Why would you say that?" He countered, somewhat irritated. "Because you're 102 years old," I said. "Yes," he said, "you're right" He stayed in bed all the next day. That night, I suggested to my son and daughter that we sit up with him through the night. He appreciated it, he said, though at one point, apparently seeing us look gloomy, he said: "I would like to make an announcement. No one in this room is dead yet." An hour or so later, he spoke his last words: "I want you to know," he said, clearly and lucidly, "that I am in no pain. I am very comfortable. And I have had as happy a life as anyone on this earth could ever have." A short time later, he died.

I miss him a lot, and I think about him a lot. I've wondered now and then how it was that my family and I were so lucky that he lived so long. I can't figure out if it was because he walked through life, or because he quit taking left turns. "Life is too short to wake up with regrets. So love the people who treat you right. Forget about the ones who don't.

Believe everything happens for a reason. If you get a chance, take it & if it changes your life, let it. Nobody said life would be easy, they just promised it would most likely be worth it."

"ENJOY LIFE NOW - IT HAS AN EXPIRATION DATE!"

Michael Gartner

I hate the words "Happy Holidays!" This is the equivalent of a doctor telling you "you have a sickness" without telling you what that sickness is.

My "holiday" is Christmas, and your holiday might be something else, and I will not be offended if you wish me a happy "whatever your day might be," so don't be offended when I say "Merry Christmas," because on that day I want you to be happy. It is not wrong for me to want you to be happy 365 days a year. I can also wish you a happy birthday, a happy Saturday, etc. etc. Understand?

Norb Svanascini

"When telling the truth, make sure you have one foot on the stirrup."

Spanish proverb

"There are some things more painful than the truth, but I can't think of any."

Norb Svanascini

TRUTH

Truth might be ugly,
Truth might hurt,
But nevertheless,
It's still the truth.

Mankind has traveled
Far and wide,
But the challenge
Has always been the same.

Truth has been the enemy
Of every despot in history,
From then, until now,
So know this my friend,

You'll be lonely,
You'll be laughed at,
But in your heart,
You'll know the truth,
When things fall apart.

Norb Svanascini

"The men who do the most with their lives are those who approach human existence, its opportunities and its problems - even in rough moments - with a confident attitude and an enthusiastic point of view."

Norman Vincent Peale

A Poem for William

A child, so innocent and beautiful
Born on the 25th day in the midst of January's cold.
So perfect and pure, not yet influenced or in need of anything
Except for nourishment and sleep.
May he always keep his pureness and spirit
And have the inner-strength to fend off the negativity and inde-
cency
That, undoubtedly, as he goes through life, will come his way.
His name is William, a name of warriors and intellects alike.
And with this short and sweet ballad, my we all
Celebrate the birth of a boy we'll call Billy,
And wish him joy and success as he starts his own Journey,
In this world we call Life.

Shawn Griffin

"Of all the times I saw my uncles, aunt, Grandparents or other family members, I cannot recall what any one of them wore, I do however remember how uniquely each one of them hugged and kissed me."

Norb Svanascini

At a fundraising dinner for a school that serves children with learning disabilities, the father of one of the students delivered a speech that would never be forgotten by all who attended. After extolling the school and its dedicated staff, he offered a question:

"When not interfered with by outside influences, everything nature does, is done with perfection. Yet my son, Shay, cannot learn things as other children do. He cannot understand things as other children do. Where is the natural order of things in my son?" The audience was stilled by the query. The father continued. "I believe that when a child like Shay, who was mentally and physically disabled, comes into the world, an opportunity to realize true human nature presents itself, and it comes in the way other people treat that child."

Then he told the following story: "Shay and I had walked past a park where some boys Shay knew were playing baseball. Shay asked, 'Do you think they'll let me play?' I knew that most of the boys would not want someone like Shay on their team, but as a father I also understood that if my son were allowed to play, it would give him a much-needed sense of belonging and some confidence to be accepted by others in spite of his handicaps. I approached one of the boys on the field and asked (not expecting much) if Shay could play. The boy looked around for guidance and said, 'We're losing by six runs and the game is in the eighth inning. I guess he can be on our team and we'll try to put him in to bat in the ninth inning.'

Shay struggled over to the team's bench and, with a broad smile, put on a team shirt. I watched with a small tear in my eye and warmth in my heart. The boys saw my joy at my son being accepted. In the bottom of the eighth inning, Shay's team scored a few runs but was still behind by three. In the top of the ninth inning, Shay put on a glove and played in the right field. Even though no hits came his way, he was obviously ecstatic just to be in the game and on the field, grinning from ear to ear as I waved to him from the stands. In the bottom of the ninth inning, Shay's team scored again. Now, with two outs and the bases loaded, the potential winning run was on base and Shay was scheduled to be next at bat.

At this juncture, do they let Shay bat and give away their chance to win the game? Surprisingly, Shay was given the bat. Everyone knew that a hit was all but impossible because Shay didn't even know how to hold the bat properly, much less connect with the ball. However, as Shay stepped up to the plate, the pitcher, recognizing that the other team was putting winning aside for this moment in Shay's life, moved in a few steps to lob the ball in softly so Shay could at least make contact. The first pitch came and Shay swung clumsily and missed.

The pitcher again took a few steps forward to toss the ball softly towards Shay. As the pitch came in, Shay swung at the ball and hit a slow ground ball right back to the pitcher.
The game would now be over. The pitcher picked up the soft grounder and could have easily thrown the ball to the first baseman. Shay would have been out and that would have been the end of the game. Instead, the pitcher threw the ball right over the first baseman's head, out of reach of all team mates.

Everyone from the stands and both teams started yelling, 'Shay, run to first! Run to first!' Never in his life had Shay ever run that far, but he made it to first base. He scampered down the baseline, wide-eyed and startled. Everyone yelled, 'Run to second, run to second!' Catching his breath, Shay awkwardly ran towards second, gleaming and struggling to make it to the base. By the time Shay rounded towards second base, the right fielder had the ball.

The smallest guy on their team who now had his first chance to be the hero for his team.

He could have thrown the ball to the second-baseman for the tag, but he understood the pitcher's intentions so he, too, intentionally threw the ball high and far over the third-baseman's head. Shay ran toward third base deliriously as the runners ahead of him circled the bases toward home. All were screaming, 'Shay, Shay, Shay, all the Way Shay'
Shay reached third base because the opposing shortstop ran to help him by turning him in the direction of third base, and shouted, 'Run to third! Shay, run to third!'

As Shay rounded third, the boys from both teams, and the spectators, were on their feet screaming, 'Shay, run home! Run home!' Shay ran to home, stepped on the plate, and was cheered as the hero who hit the grand slam and won the game for his team."

"That day," said the father softly with tears now rolling down his face, "the boys from both teams helped bring a piece of true love and humanity into this world. Shay didn't make it to another summer. He died that winter, having never forgotten being the hero and making me so happy and coming home and seeing his Mother tearfully embrace her little hero of the day!"

Author Unknown

It was one morning like any other. I, as I often am, in a bad mood. I complained because you were taking too much time to have breakfast. I yelled because you were playing with the cutlery and I got upset because you chewed with your mouth open.

You started goofing around and then spilled milk on your clothes. Furious, I scolded you again and told you to shape up immediately.

On the way to school we didn't speak. Sitting in the seat of the car you seemed lost. I warned you to be good and to behave yourself in school.

In the afternoon, when I returned home after a day of hard work, I found you playing in the garden. Your new pants had stains and were dirty and wet.

In front of your friends I told you that you had to take care of your clothing and shoes; that parents made the sacrifice to dress you well.
I told you to get in the house and change your clothes and, before you went upstairs, I told you to walk straight.

Later, you were making noise and running around the house.

At dinner, I threw my napkin on the table and I stood up furiously because you would not stop horsing around. I pounded my fist on the table and I went to my room.

Soon my anger began to diminish. I realized that I was being too harsh and I wanted to go down to give you a hug but I couldn't.

How could a father, after making such a scene, admit that he was wrong?

Then I heard a tapping at the door. "Come in," I said, guessing that it was my him.

He opened the door slowly and stood by the door. I looked at him seriously and asked, "Are you going to sleep?" You came to tell me good night?"

He did not answer. He walked slowly with those small steps and waited for me to take him into my arms. I hugged him… and with a lump in the throat I perceived the lightness of his slim body.

His small arms were around my neck and he gave me a kiss gently on the cheek. "I felt that in my soul."

"See you in the morning Daddy," he told me.
What was I doing? Why did I get upset so easily? I treated him as an adult person. I wanted him to be like me and we certainly weren't equal.

He had some qualities which I lacked: He is legitimate, pure, good, and above all, knows how to show love.

Why is it hard for me to understand? Why do I have the habit of being always angry? Why don't I have more patience? I was also a boy. When did I start to change?

After a while I went to your room and carefully lit a lamp. You were sound asleep. Your beautiful face was pink. Your mouth, half open. You looked like a baby, my baby.
I leaned over to touch your cheek with my lips; I took a breath of your clean and fresh scent. I could not contain the tears and

closed my eyes. One of my tears fell on your skin. You did not notice

I got on my knees and I asked for forgiveness in silence. I carefully covered him with the blankets and left the room. If God listens to me and lets you live many years, someday you'll know that parents are not perfect. But above all, I hope you realize that, despite all my mistakes, I love you more than my life.

Author Unknown

While a man was polishing his new car, his 4 year old son picked up a stone and scratched lines on the side of the car. In anger, the man took the child's hand and hit it many times, not realizing he was using a wrench.

At the hospital, the child lost all his fingers due to multiple fractures. When the child saw his father, with painful eyes he asked, "Dad when will my fingers grow back?" The man was so hurt and speechless; he went back to his car and kicked it a lot of times.

Devastated by his own actions… sitting in front of that car he looked at the scratches; the child had written "LOVE YOU DAD." The next day that man committed suicide…

END

Anger and Love have no limits; choose the latter to have a beautiful, lovely life… Things are to be used and people are to be loved but, the problem in today's world is, people are used and things are loved…

During this year, let's be careful to keep this thought in mind: Things are to be used… People are to be loved… Be yourself… This is the only day we HAVE. Have a nice day.

Watch your thoughts; they become words. Watch your words; they become actions.

Watch your actions; they become habits. Watch your habits they become character;

Watch your character; it becomes your destiny.

Author Unknown

I was 11, only child, all friends left behind, different language, different customs, in short, really alone. My father buys an encyclopedia, a Britannica; it becomes my friend at the right moment. I read it constantly, any subject; every page becomes a mystery that becomes unraveled. I become recognized not because of sports but for a fountain of varied areas of knowledge. I still have my friend in a special place in my library. Today, Encyclopedia Britannica ceased production of its printed edition. The next 11 year old that finds himself alone in a new world will not have that book to caress when he needs it the most.

I do not know what a father can get his son today that can replace that.

Norb Svanascini

There was a young woman who had been diagnosed with a terminal illness and had been given three months to live. So, as she was getting her things "in order," she contacted her Pastor and had him come to her house to discuss certain aspects of her final wishes.

She told him which songs she wanted sung at the service, what scriptures she would like read, and what outfit she wanted to be buried in.

Everything was in order and the Pastor was preparing to leave when the young woman suddenly remembered something very important to her. "There's one more thing," she said excitedly.
"What's that?" came the Pastor's reply.
"This is very important," the young woman continued. "I want to be buried with a fork in my right hand."

The Pastor stood looking at the young woman, not knowing quite what to say. "That surprises you, doesn't it?" the young woman asked.

"Well, to be honest, I'm puzzled by the request," said the Pastor.

The young woman explained. "My grandmother once told me this story and from that time on I have always tried to pass along its message to those I love and those who are in need of encouragement. In all my years of attending socials and dinners, I always remember when the dishes of the main course were being cleared; someone would inevitably lean over and say, 'Keep your fork.' It was my favorite part because I knew that something better was coming... like velvety chocolate cake or deep-dish apple pie.

Something wonderful and with substance! So, I just want people to see me there in that casket with a fork in my hand and I want them to wonder 'What's with the fork?' Then I want you to tell them: 'Keep your fork, the best is yet to come.'

The Pastor's eyes welled up with tears of joy as he hugged the young woman good-bye. He knew this would be one of the last times he would see her before her death. But he also knew that the young woman had a better grasp of heaven than he did. She had a better grasp of what heaven would be like than many people twice her age, with twice as much experience and knowledge. She KNEW that something better was coming.

At the funeral, people were walking by the young woman's casket and they saw the cloak she was wearing and the fork placed in her right hand. Over and over, the Pastor heard the question, "What's with the fork?" And over and over he smiled.

During his message, the Pastor told the people of the conversation he had with the young woman shortly before she died. He also told them about the fork and about what it symbolized to her. He told everyone that he could not stop thinking about the fork and told them they probably would not be able to stop thinking about it either.

He was right.

So, the next time you reach down for your fork let it remind you, ever so gently, that the best is yet to come. Friends are a very rare jewel, indeed. They make you smile and encourage you to succeed Cherish the time you have, and the memories you share...

being friends with someone is not an opportunity, but a sweet responsibility.

And just remember...keep your fork!

Author Unknown

In life, you are either in camp #1 or camp #2

Camp #1: You know you know very little, never end your search for the truth, wherever it takes you, even if it's ugly or against everything you've been taught.

Camp#2: You believe what you've been taught.

Norb Svanascini

THIS I BELIEVE

"100 years from now it will not matter what my bank account was the sort of house I live then or the kind of car I drove but the world may be different because I was important in the life of a boy."

Boy Scouts motto

"Self conquest is the greatest of victories."

Plato

My Most Memorable Birthday

Someone asked me which present that was given to me in my lifetime, did I remember the most. Only one do I remember more than others, maybe because life is much simpler at that age, and desires are simpler to please.

As a young boy of 8 years I was allowed to have a Coke a day---no more.

Back then they were 6 ounce bottles; it never seemed enough.

My parents asked what I wanted for my birthday, and without hesitation, I answered: a case of Coke, and I want to drink as many as I want.

My birthday came and my wish was granted. I took my first bottle and could not wait until I could open my second; after the second, which was enough to satisfy any 8 year old, I could not resist the opportunity of opening a third bottle.

I have forgotten whether I finished it or not ,but I do remember laying down in a bench enjoying this moment of pure bliss.

Norb Svanascini

"Ninety-nine percent of the failures come from people who have the habit of making excuses."

George Washington

"I know that most men, including those at ease with problems of the greatest complexity, can seldom accept even the simplest and most obvious truth if it be such as would oblige them to admit the falsity of conclusions which they have delighted in explaining to colleagues, which they have proudly taught to others, and which they have woven, thread by thread, into the fabric of their lives."

Leo Tolstoy

"Evil is the desire to have power over other human beings."

Norb Svanascini

THOUGHTS ON ABORTION

"The argument that is the most used as a pro abortion excuse is " it's my body and I have the right to choose". Well let me tell you: when that fetus starts developing as a child, after conception, it is an independent being, it ceases to be part of the woman's body. This is not an appendix or a gall bladder, this is an independent human who is not part of this woman, but is only being fed and nurtured by this host."

Norb Svanascini

"Abortion is an irresponsible act to rectify another irresponsible act, and we all know since we are small children that two wrongs don't make a right."

Norb Svanascini

"You can forget all the discussions about abortion you've heard up to now. The one that has never been discussed is that a woman, being the foundation of societies, the one common denominator of structure in the family, when convinced that she can actually kill a living being within her, is also the beginning of the end of that society she belongs to."

Norb Svanascini

"Discovering the truth about ourselves is a lifetime's work, but it's worth the effort."

Fred Rogers

"Stopping at third base adds no more to the score than striking out."

E. Joseph Cossman

FRIENDS

I read a story that should be read by everyone, here it is :
One day, when I was a freshman in high school. I saw a kid from my class was walking home from school. His name was Kyle. It looked like he was carrying all of his books.

I thought to myself, 'Why would anyone bring home all his books on a Friday?

He must really be a nerd. I had quite a weekend planned (parties and a football game with my friends tomorrow afternoon), so I shrugged my shoulders and went on. As I was walking, I saw a bunch of kids running toward him. They ran at him, knocking all his books out of his arms and tripping him so he landed in the dirt. His glasses went flying, and I saw them land in the grass about ten feet from him. He looked up and I saw this terrible sadness in his eyes; my heart went out to him, so I jogged over to him as he crawled around looking for his glasses, and I saw a tear in his eye. As I handed him his glasses, I said, 'Those guys are jerks. They really should get lives.

He looked at me and said, 'Hey thanks!' There was a big smile on his face. It was one of those smiles that showed real gratitude. I helped him pick up his books, and asked him where he lived. As it turned out, he lived near me, so I asked him why I had never seen him before. He said he had gone to private school before now. I would have never hung out with a private school kid before. We talked all the way home, and I carried some of his books. He turned out to be a pretty cool kid. I asked him if he wanted to play a little football with my friends, He said yes.

We hung out all weekend and the more I got to know Kyle, the more I liked him, and my friends thought the same of him. Monday morning came, and there was Kyle with the huge stack of books again. I stopped him and said, 'Boy, you are gonna really build some serious muscles with this pile of books everyday!' He just laughed and handed me half the books. Over the next four years, Kyle and I became best friends...When we were seniors we began to think about college. Kyle decided on Georgetown and I was going to Duke. I knew that we would always be friends, that the miles would never be a problem. He was going to be a doctor and I was going for business on a football scholarship. Kyle was valedictorian of our class. I teased him all the time about being a nerd. He had to prepare a speech for graduation. I was so glad it wasn't me having to get up there and speak. Graduation day, I saw Kyle. He looked great.

He was one of those guys that really found himself during high school. He filled out and actually looked good in glasses. He had more dates than I had, and all the girls loved him. Boy, sometimes I was jealous! Today was one of those days. I could see that he was nervous about his speech. So, I smacked him on the back and said, 'Hey, big guy, you'll be great!' He looked at me with one of those looks (the really grateful one) and smiled. ' Thanks,' he said. As he started his speech, he cleared his throat, and began 'Graduation is a time to thank those who helped you make it through those tough years. Your parents, your teachers, your siblings, maybe a coach...but mostly your friends...I am here to tell all of you that being a friend to someone is the best gift you can give them..I am going to tell you a story.'

I just looked at my friend with disbelief as he told the story of the first day we met. He had planned to kill himself over the weekend. He talked of how he had cleaned out his locker so his Mom wouldn't have to do it later and was carrying his stuff home. He looked hard at me and gave me a little smile. 'Thankfully, I was saved. My friend saved me from doing the unspeakable.'I heard the gasp go through the crowd as this handsome, popular boy told us all about his weakest moment.

I saw his Mom and dad looking at me and smiling that same grateful smile. Not until that moment did I realize it's depth. Never underestimate the power of your actions. With one small gesture you can change a person's life. For better or for worse. God puts us all in each others lives to impact one another in some way.

'Friends are angels who lift us to our feet when our wings have trouble remembering how to fly.' There is no beginning or end.. Yesterday is history. Tomorrow is a mystery. Today is a gift.

Author Unknown

"The quality of a person's life is in direct proportion to their commitment to excellence, regardless of their chosen field of endeavor."

Vincent Lombardi

"Every morning in Africa, a gazelle wakes up. It knows it must run faster than the fastest lion or it will be killed...Every morning a lion wakes up. It knows it must outrun the slowest gazelle or it will starve to death. It doesn't matter whether you are a lion or a gazelle...when the sun comes up, you'd better be running."

Author Unknown

"The reasonable man adapts himself to the world; the unreasonable one persists in trying to adapt the world to himself. Therefore all progress depends on the unreasonable man."

George Bernard Shaw

"As we travel in this adventure called life, you must be careful about the decisions you make, this gift that has been given to you is a life full of wonders, that if done properly, not only will give you constant happiness, but will also explain the meaning of life itself."

Norb Svanascini

Growing up in Southern Indiana gave me a lot of great memories, but the one that I remember with the greatest pleasure was a man by the name of Wendell McNay.

Maybe it's because the age I had become, or maybe it was because of my love of cars , but at 16 and having a car , I believe there are very few people that reach that level of happiness.

Unluckily at that age you do a lot of stupid things, and the most common one is to wreck your car.

Here you are, with your most prized possession , bent fender , twisted bumper, and damaged (beyond repair) tire. No money and your parents, probably happy that it's only this small, are not going to help you so you'll learn your lesson. You talk to your friends, and one of them tells you : go see Wendell McNay, he'll help you.

Now let me tell you about Wendell McNay: when I was 16 he must have been 65-70 which at that time it seemed as he was older than just about anybody; he had a permanent camel cigarette soaked half way down , and if was ever lit , I never saw it. He was dressed in black overalls that were always covered with dust/paint/mud.

His office was one of those offices that you do not want to go into because you knew you would contract some kind of terminal disease.

Wendell, as he insisted everyone call him had a very good auto body shop , but he would take the time to help every teenager that was either customizing his car, or who had wrecked it ; he didn't care if he did any of the work , he just helped you.

He was ,as very few people are , genuine. The first thing he taught you is where the scrap yards were , and which one would be the best one to go to; furthermore he would tell you how much to pay for this , and even taught you how to deal with the scrap yard owner. After the gathering of the necessary parts , Wendell would tell you how to remove and replace the damaged parts correctly, at this point if you did it right, he would ok it , if not he would tell you to take it all apart and re-do it even if it was all done, and he made sure you did it yourself, after that you drove more carefully, in short, you matured.

The shame of growing up and forgetting these incredible people, is that you do not appreciate it until they're gone, but these are the people that leave that lasting impression you never forget, that you, whether you know it or not, you try to emulate .

So please, learn to identify these people that will leave an impact that will affect all your life, in the way you treat other people, and also setting the standard by which you will always judge excellence. Let them know now how much you appreciate them.

Norb Svanascini

Tears

You never know what may cause them. The sight of an ocean can do it, a piece of music, a newborn, a scene from a movie you've seen before. They are the result of happiness or sadness, depending where you are at that moment; whether the national anthem is played, or witnessing a tragedy, you can never be sure when they happen; but of this you can be sure, whenever you find tears in your eyes, especially unexpected tears, it is well to pay close attention.

Tears tell you something about the secret that you are, but more often than not,God is speaking to you through them, revealing the mystery of where you really come from, and at the same time showing you where to go if your soul is to be saved, where to go next.

Frederick Buechner

GO to the people
LIVE among the people
LEARN from them
LOVE them.
START with what they know,
BUILD on what they have.
But of the BEST leaders,
When their TASK is accomplished,
Their WORK is done,
The PEOPLE will remark,
"WE HAVE DONE IT OURSELVES"

Lao Tzu

WHERE CHARACTER IS EVERYTHING

There's a place where royalty meets peasants, where color doesn't matter, where education is irrelevant, whether you're tall or short, man or woman, it doesn't matter.

There is a place where character is everything. There's a place where your word is a contract, where a contract is a contract, that no amount of lawyers can overturn.

There is a place where a man has to be a man, where even a woman has to be a man.

There,s a place where when you win, you win, and when you lose, you lose, and when you lose, you know you've lost, and when you win, you know you've won, and after you've won, you get up, and for that moment, you know you were the best.

Getting up from the table, you take a feeling with you that you'll always cherish, because you know that through a combination of good decisions, a little luck, and a bad move from some of your opponents when they had you beat, that at that moment, you are the best at Texas Hold'em.

Norb Svanascini

"Ideals are like stars. You will not succeed in touching them with your hands; but like the seafaring man, you choose them as your guides, and following them, you will reach your destiny."

Carl Schurz

"Life's journey is not to arrive at the grave safely in a well preserved body, but rather to skid in sideways, totally used up and worn out, shouting '...man, what a ride!"

George Carlin

"I only wish that God gave me the ability to match the expectations of the people I know and trust me."

Norb Svanascini

"The real measure of your wealth is how much you would be worth if you lost all of your money."

Author Unknown

RECOMMENDED MOVIES

My Life
It's a Wonderful Life
Dr. Zhivago
Kings Row
Mr Deeds Goes to Town
Zorba the Greek
Pride of the Yankees

CHAPTER 8

WISDOM

"Most of us don't know about happiness until it's over."

Claudette Colbert

"I tell you that virtue is not given by money, but that from virtue come money and every other good of man, public as well as private."

Socrates

"It is hard to see how a great man can be an atheist. Without the sustaining influence of faith in a divine power we could have little faith in ourselves. We need to feel that behind us is intelligence and love. Doubters do not achieve; skeptics do not contribute; cynics do not create. Faith is the great motive power, and no man realizes his full possibilities unless he has the deep conviction that life is eternally important, and that his work, well done, is a part of an unending plan."

Calvin Coolidge

"It's amazing what people plant in their own head."

Art Sbarounis

L ive life for The Moment. You don't know when it's going to come. It may happen at night. Or during the day. Keep your ears and eyes open to it. Embrace it with every ounce of energy in your mind and body because you don't want to miss it. It may not happen until you're 85 years old, or it may have happened to you when you were 5 years old.

The Moment doesn't know time. Time doesn't understand nor care about The Moment. The Moment doesn't care about your age. And neither should you. It may be a short, sweet kiss. It may come when you are not expecting it, so keep your heart awake. It may cause you to marry. It may cause you to cry. It may make you crazy. Don't be afraid. Embrace it.

Because when The Moment comes, it touches your heart like nothing else can. It makes your heart sing. It makes your heart strong. Let love into your heart, because it won't give you notice, The Moment it touches you. It's the greatest feeling this life can give you, so don't miss it.

Norb Svanascini

"You can only perceive real beauty in a person as they get older."

Anouk Aimee

Do more than exist, live.
Do more than look, observe.
Do more than read, absorb.
Do more than hear, listen.
Do more than listen, understand.
Do more than think, ponder.
Do more than plan, act.
Do more than talk, say something.

John H. Rhoades

Do not fear the enemy, for your enemy can only take your life. It is far better that you fear the media, for they will steal your HONOR. That awful power, the public opinion of a nation, is created in America by a horde of ignorant, self-complacent simpletons who failed at ditching and shoemaking and fetched up in journalism on their way to the poorhouse.

Mark Twain

"A pessimist sees the difficulty in every opportunity; an optimist sees the opportunity in every difficulty."

Winston Churchill

"The secret of success is contained in the name of that famous Spanish painter. GOYA."

"As I approve of a youth that has something of the old man in him, so I am no less pleased with an old man that has something of the youth. He that follows this rule may be old in body, but can never be so in mind. "

Marcus Tullius Cicero

"If you want a real simple formula to find out what's really important, try this out:
What could you live without? Water? Air? Food? How about an Armani suit? A Rolex?
Get it?"

Norb Svanascini

"Pity the person who knows the price of everything, and the value of nothing."

Norb Svanascini

A man can lose many things,
Some he can recover,
But one thing, I can assure you,
And it's good for you to know,
If you ever lose your shame,
You'll never find it again

Martin Fierro
Gaucho philosopher

"The function of wisdom is to discriminate between good and evil."
Marcus Tullius Cicero

"To see a world in a Grain of Sand,
And a Heaven in a Wild Flower,
Hold Infinity in the palm of your hand,
And Eternity in an hour."

William Blake

The thought manifests as the word;
The word manifests as the deed;
The deed develops into habit;
And habit hardens into character;
So watch the thought and its ways with care,
And let it spring from love
Born out of concern for all beings…
As the shadow follows the body,
As we think, so we become.

Buddha
Dhammapada

"If you knew what I know about the power of giving, you would not let a single meal pass without sharing it in some way."
Buddha

183

"Time is like a river that will take you forward into encounters with reality that will require you to make decisions. You can't stop the movement down this river and you can't avoid the encounters. You can only approach these encounters in the best way possible."

Ray Dalio

"Nothing in the world can take the place of Persistence. Talent will not; nothing is more common than unsuccessful men with talent. Genius will not; unrewarded genius is almost a proverb. Education will not; the world is full of educated derelicts. Persistence and determination alone are omnipotent. The slogan 'Press On' has solved and always will solve the problems of the human race."

Calvin Coolidge

"Life should not be a journey to the grave with the intention of arriving safely in a pretty and well preserved body, but rather to skid in broadside in a cloud of smoke, thoroughly used up, totally worn out, and loudly proclaiming 'Wow! What a Ride!'"

Hunter S. Thompson
The Proud Highway: Saga of a Desperate Southern Gentleman

"How can something so narrow, be so deep as a woman?"

Norb Svanascini

Sadness so deep that oceans are envious
Sadness that only a loss of something real can produce
Sadness that you can only hope, that someday, will disappear.

Norb Svanascini

"There is no foundation like the rock of honesty and fairness, and when you begin to build your life on that rock, combined with the cement of a faith in God, then you have a real start."

Barry Goldwater

"He has all of the virtues I dislike and none of the vices I admire."

Winston Churchill

"If you want to really know a person, don't ask what they do, ask what they are passionate about. This will unlock the way to their inner self."

Norb Svanascini

*"Nothing is as strong as gentleness,
And nothing is so gentle as real strength."*

Ralph W. Sockman

"The giant oak is an acorn that held its ground."

Author Unknown

"Love all, trust a few. Do wrong to none."

William Shakespeare

"The most powerful weapon on earth is the human soul on fire."

Ferdinand Foch

*"The strength of a family is like the strength of an army.
It depends on the loyalty to each other."*

Mario Puzo

*"Life is not about waiting for the storms to pass...
It's about learning how to dance in the rain!"*

Vivian Greene

Legend has it that one evening an old Cherokee told his grandson about a battle that goes on inside people. He said, "My son, the battle is between two wolves inside us all.

One is Evil. It is anger, envy, jealousy, sorrow, regret, greed, arrogance, self-pity, guilt, resentment, inferiority, lies, false pride, superiority, and ego.

The other is Good. It is joy, peace, love, hope, serenity, humility, kindness, benevolence, empathy, generosity, truth, compassion and faith."

The grandson thought about it for a minute and then asked his grandfather: "Which wolf wins?" The old Cherokee replied, "The one you feed."

Author Unknown

"Happy is the man who has broken the chains which hurt the mind, and has given up worrying once and for all."

Ovid

"It's not hard to make decisions when you know what your values are."

Roy E. Disney
Nephew of Walt Disney

"All truths are easy to understand once they are discovered.
The point is to discover them."

Galileo

"Chances are right now you are standing in your own acres of diamonds."
Earl Nightingale

There are times in everyone's life when something constructive is born out of adversity.

There are times that things seem so bad that you've got to grasp your fate by the shoulders and shake it.

In times of stress and adversity, it's always best to keep busy, to plow your anger and your energy into something quite positive.

Lee Iacocca

What we do as poker players is read people. People lie to us; they try to bluff us constantly. So we get used to trying to sort out all the bullsh**. When I get pitched by people who are really good, like con men, they are not as good as the poker players.

You can't cheat an honest man. I don't know exactly why that is, but it's true for me. My honor is unquestioned in poker, and if you have perfect honor in poker, it's better than having it anywhere elsc in life because everyone remembers everything from 15 or 20 years ago. If you cheated then, they'll remember.

Phil Hellmuth
Poker World Champion

It is not the critic who counts; not the man who points out how the strong man stumbles, or where the doer of deeds could have done them better. The credit belongs to the man who is actually in the arena, whose face is marred by dust and sweat and blood; who strives valiantly; who errs, who comes short again and again, because there is no effort without error and shortcoming; but who does actually strive to do the deeds; who knows great enthusiasms, the great devotions; who spends himself in a worthy cause; who at the best knows in the end the triumph of high achievement, and who at the worst, if he fails, at least fails while daring greatly, so that his place shall never be with those cold and timid souls who neither know victory nor defeat.

Theodore Roosevelt

Life does not consist mainly, or even largely, of facts or happenings. It consists mainly of the storm of thoughts that is forever flowing through one's head."

Mark Twain

"My life has been filled with terrible misfortune; most of which never happened."

Michel Eyquem de Montaigne

"Life is what happens to us while we are making other plans."

Thomas La Mance

"There are two things to aim at in life: first, to get what you want; and, after that, to enjoy it. Only the wisest of mankind achieve the second."

Logan Pearsall Smith

"He has achieved success who has lived well, laughed often, and loved much."

Bessie Anderson Stanley

"Show me a guy who's afraid to look bad and I will show you a guy you can beat every time."

Lou Brock

"Be very, very careful what you put into that head, because you will never, ever get it out."

Thomas Cardinal Wolsey
(1471-1530)

"Believe nothing, no matter where you read it, or who said it, no matter if I have said it, unless it agrees with your own reason and your common sense."

Buddha

"Genius ain't anything more than elegant common sense."

Josh Billing

"There is no revenge so complete as forgiveness."

Josh Billings

Twenty years from now you will be more disappointed by the things you didn't do than by the ones you did do. So throw off the bowlines. Sail away from the safe harbor. Catch the trade winds in your sails. Explore. Dream. Discover.

Mark Twain

"There is more truth in a 5 year old's observations than there is at Harvard."

Norb Svanascini

"The freedom of mankind rests on man's ability to mind their own business, and if this is ever achieved, which is doubtful, then there will be peace."

Norb Svanascini

There are a lot of things in the world that cannot be bought with money. These are Honor, Honesty, and Integrity. You will be inundated with people that are admired because other people treat them as if they deserve these traits, but don't be fooled; most of these people are not worthy recipients of the accolades they receive.

Look at a person of what they've created, how they treat other people, especially the ones that he or she doesn't have to impress, like a waitress, or a worker.

The person who is striving to achieve these qualities knows what they really are, and does not need anyone else to recognize them.

Norb Svanascini

"Money doesn't change people, it only exposes them."

Norb Svanascini

"The only thing we learn from history, I am afraid, is that we do not learn from history."

Ron Paul

"That which you covet makes you weak."

Norb Svanascini

"Am I therefore become your enemy, because I tell you the truth?"

Galatians 4:16

"Political correctness is an intellectual inquisition."

Norb Svanascini

"There are some ideas so absurd that only an intellectual could believe them."

George Orwell

"Insanity is often defined as repeating the same action while expecting a different result."

Albert Einstein

"Drunkenness is temporary suicide."

Bertrand Russell

A lady in a faded gingham dress and her husband, dressed in a homespun threadbare suit, stepped off the train in Boston, and walked timidly without an appointment into the Harvard University President's outer office. The secretary could tell in a moment that such backwoods, country hicks had no business at

Harvard and probably didn't even deserve to be in Cambridge
"We want to see the president," the man said softly.
"He'll be busy all day," the secretary snapped.
" We'll wait," the lady replied.

For hours the secretary ignored them, hoping that the couple would finally become discouraged and go away. They didn't and the secretary grewfrustrated and finally decided to disturb the president, even though it was a chore she always regretted. "Maybe if you see them for a few minutes, they'll leave," she said to him. He sighed in exasperation and nodded. Someone of his importance obviously didn't have the time to spend with them, but he detested gingham dresses and homespun suits cluttering up his outer office. The president, stern faced and with dignity, strutted toward the couple.

The lady told him, "We had a son who attended Harvard for one year. He loved Harvard. He was happy here. But about a year ago, he was accidentally killed. My husband and I would like to erect a memorial to him, somewhere on campus."

The president wasn't touched.... He was shocked. "Madam," he said, gruffly, "we can't put up a statue for every person who attended Harvard and died. If we did, this place would look like a cemetery."

'[Oh, no," the lady explained quickly. "We don't want to erect a statue. We thought we would like to give a building to Harvard."

The president rolled his eyes. He glanced at the gingham dress and homespun suit, then exclaimed, "A building! Do you have any earthly idea how much a building costs? We have over seven and a half million dollars in the physical buildings here at Harvard."

For a moment the lady was silent. The president was pleased. Maybe he could get rid of them now.

The lady turned to her husband and said quietly, "Is that all it costs to start a university? Why don't we just start our own?" Her husband nodded. The president's face wilted in confusion and bewilderment.

Mr. and Mrs. Leland Stanford got up and walked away, traveling to Palo Alto, California where they established the university that bears their name, Stanford University, a memorial to a son that Harvard no longer cared about.

You can easily judge the character of others by how they treat those who they think can do nothing.
A TRUE STORY

Malcolm Forbes

"What lies behind us and what lies before us are tiny matters compared to what lies within us."

Henry S. Haskins

"The more a man knows, the more he forgives."

Confucius

"There are only two ways to live your life: as though nothing is a miracle, or as though everything is a miracle."

Albert Einstein

"If you have a garden and a library, you have everything you need."

Marcus Tullius Cicero

"Someone's sitting in the shade today because someone planted a tree a long time ago."

Warren Buffet

"Human subtlety will never devise an invention more beautiful, more simple or more direct than does nature because in her inventions nothing is lacking, and nothing is superfluous."

Leonardo da Vinci

"When I left my house, still a child, my mother accompanied me to the station and when I boarded the train she said, 'This is the second and last gift I can give you: the first gift was to give you life, the second gift, is the freedom to live it.'"

Facundo Cabral

"You have been given a brain just like Einstein, you have a heart like Jesus, you have two hands like Mother Teresa, you have a will, same as Moses, You have a soul like Gandhi, and you have been given a spirit as the Buddha. So tell me, how can you feel poor and miserable? "

Facundo Cabral

"If we are not ashamed to think it, we should not be ashamed to say it."

Marcus Tullius Cicero

All Fords are exactly alike, but no two men are just alike. Every new life is a new thing under the sun; there has never been anything just like it before, never will be again. A young man ought to get that idea about himself; he should look for the single spark of individuality that makes him different from other folks, and develop that for all he is worth. Society and schools may try to iron it out of him; their tendency is to put it all in the same mold, but I say don't let that spark be lost; it is your only real claim to importance."

Henry Ford

"Those who can make you believe absurdities, can make you commit atrocities."

Voltaire

"It is possible to move mountains or to change the course of a river the hardest thing on earth is to change the way of a person."

Liin Yu Tan

"Wealth it's not what you have, but what you can do with the things around you."

Quote found on a Japanese garden

Two friends were walking through the desert. During their journey they had an argument, and one friend slapped the other in the face.

The one who was slapped was hurt, but without saying anything, he wrote in the sand: "Today my best friend slapped me in the face."

They kept on walking until they found an oasis, where they decided to take a bath. The one who had been slapped got stuck in the mire and started drowning, but his friend saved him.

After he recovered, he wrote on a stone: "Today my best friend saved my life."

The friend who had slapped, and saved his best friend asked him: "After I hurt you, you wrote in the sand and now you write on a stone. Why?"

The other friend replied: "When someone hurts us we should write it down in the sand where the winds of forgiveness can erase it. But when someone does something good for us, we must engrave it in stone where no wind can ever remove it."

Learn to write your hurts in the sand and to carve your benefits in stone. It only takes a minute to find a special person, an hour to appreciate them, a day to love them, but an entire life to forget them. Remember to truly appreciate your special friends and let them know how much you care.

Author Unknown

Easiest Things in the World

My father always told me that the two easiest things in the world are:

1. Spend money--you can teach a monkey to do this.

2. Be a critic--people doing this are the missing link between man and monkeys.

"He who is plenteously provided for from within, needs but little from without."

Johann Wolfgang von Goethe

Positive Attitude in Scientific Terms

Below are three astonishing experiments with DNA which proves That DNA can heal itself according to the "feelings" of the individual as reported recently by Gregg Braden. In his recent program entitled Healing Hearts/Healing Nations: The Science of Peace and the Power OF Prayer, Gregg Braden discussed how in the past we lost huge amounts of information from ancient spiritual traditions (when the library at Alexandria burned we lost at least 532,000 documents), and that there may be information in those traditions which could help us understand some of the mysteries of science. To this end he reported on three very interesting experiments. Gregg Braden started off as a scientist and engineer, before he began pursuing these larger questions.

EXPERIMENT #1

The first experiment reported was done by Dr. Vladimir Poponin, a quantum biologist. In this experiment, first a container was emptied (i.e. a vacuum was created within it), and then the only thing left photons (particles of light) they measured the distribution (i.e., the location) of the photons and found they were completely random inside the container. This was the expected result.

Then some DNA was placed inside the container and the distribution (location) of the photons was re-measured. Then some DNA was placed inside the container and the distribution (location) of the photons was re-measured.

This time the photons were LINED UP in an ORDERED way

and aligned with the DNA. In other words, the physical DNA had an effect on the non-physical photons. After that, the DNA was removed from the container, and the distribution of the photons was measured again. The photons REMAINED ORDERED and lined up where the DNA had been.

What are the light particles connected to?

Gregg Braden says we are forced to accept the possibility that some NEW field of energy, a web of energy, is there and the DNA is communicating with the photons through this energy.

EXPERIMENT #2

These were experiments done by the military.

Leukocytes (white blood cells) were collected for DNA from donors and placed into chambers so they could measure electrical changes. In this experiment, the donor was placed in one room and subjected to "emotional stimulation" consisting of video clips, which generated different emotions in the donor. The DNA was placed in a different room in the same building. Both the donor and his DNA were monitored and as the donor exhibited emotional peaks or valleys (measured by electrical responses), the DNA exhibited the IDENTICAL RESPONSES AT THE EXACT SAME TIME. There was no lag time, no transmission time. The DNA peaks and valleys EXACTLY MATCHED the peaks and valleys of the donor in time.

The military wanted to see how far away they could separate the donor from his DNA and still get this effect. They stopped testing after they separated the DNA and the donor by 50 miles and STILL had the SAME result. No lag time; no transmission time. The DNA and the donor had the same identical responses in time. What can this mean? Gregg Braden says it means that living cells communicate through a previously unrecognized form of energy. This energy is not affected by time and distance. This is a non-local form of energy, an energy that already exists everywhere, all the time.

EXPERIMENT #3

The third experiment was done by the Institute of Heart Math and the paper that was written about this was titled: Local and Non local Effects of Coherent Heart Frequencies on Conformational Changes of DNA. (Disregard the title! The info is incredible.

This is the experiment that relates directly to the anthrax situation. In this experiment, some human placenta DNA (the most pristine form of DNA) was placed in a container from which they could measure changes in the DNA. Twenty-eight vials of DNA were given (one each) to 28 trained researchers. Each researcher had been trained how to generate and FEEL feelings, and they each had strong emotions.

What was discovered was that the DNA CHANGED ITS SHAPE according to the feelings of the researchers:

1. When the researchers FELT gratitude, love and appreciation, the DNA responded by RELAXING and the strands unwound. The length of the DNA became longer.

2. When the researchers FELT anger, fear, frustration, or stress, the DNA responded by TIGHTENING UP. It became shorter and SWITCHED OFF many of our DNA codes! If you've ever felt "shut down" by negative emotions, now you know why your body was equally shut down too. The shut down of the DNA codes was reversed and the codes were switched back on again when feelings of love, joy, gratitude and appreciation were felt by the researchers.

This experiment was later followed up by testing HIV positive patients. They discovered that feelings of love, gratitude and appreciation created 300,000 TIMES the RESISTANCE they had without those feelings. So here's the answer to what can help you stay well, no matter what dreadful virus or bacteria may be floating around.

Stay in feelings of joy, love, gratitude and appreciation!

These emotional changes went beyond the effects of electro-magnetics. Individuals trained in deep love were able to change the shape of their DNA. Gregg Braden says this illustrates a new recognized form of energy that connects all of creation. This energy appears to be a TIGHTLY WOVEN WEB that connects all matter. Essentially we're able to influence this web of creation through our VIBRATION.

SUMMARY:

What do the results of these experiments have to do with our present situation? This is the science behind how we can choose a timeline to stay safe, no matter what else is happening. As Gregg explains in The Isaiah Effect, basically time is not just linear (past, present and future), but it also has depth. The depth of time consists of all the possible prayers and timelines that could ever be prayed or exist. Essentially, all our prayers have already been answered. We just activate the one we're living through our FEELINGS.

THIS is how we create our reality - by choosing it with our feelings. Our feelings are activating the timeline via the web of creation, which connects all of the energy and matter of the Universe.

Remember that the law of the Universe is that we attract what we focus on. If you are focused on fearing whatever may come, you are sending a strong message to the Universe to send you whatever you fear. Instead if you can get yourself into feelings of joy, love, appreciation or gratitude, and focus on bringing more of that into your life, you are going to avoid the negative stuff automatically.

You will be choosing a different TIMELINE with your feelings.

You can prevent getting anthrax or any other flu, virus, etc, by staying in these positive feelings, which maintains an incredibly strong immune system.

So here's your protection for whatever comes: Find something to be happy about every day, and every hour if possible, moment-to-moment, even if only for a few minutes.

Author Unknown

Recommended Movies

High Noon
Shane
One-Eyed Jacks
The Hustler
Sleepers
Serpico